It's Not Really About the Hair

It's Not Really About the Hair

The Honest Truth About

Life, Love, and the Business of Beauty

tabatha coffey

with Richard Buskin

itbooks

Chapter-opening photographs courtesy of Hama Sanders. Insert photographs courtesy of the author.

The names and identifying characteristics of some of the individuals featured throughout the book have been changed to protect their privacy.

A hardcover edition of this book was published in 2011 by It Books, an imprint of HarperCollins Publishers.

HarperCollins books may be purchased for educational, business, or sales promotional use. For information please write: Special Markets Department, HarperCollins Publishers, 10 East 53rd Street, New York, NY 10022.

FIRST IT BOOKS PAPERBACK PUBLISHED 2012.

Designed by Paula Russell Szafranski

The Library of Congress has catalogued the hardcover edition as follows:

Coffey, Tabatha, 1969-
  It's not really about the hair : the honest truth about life, love,
and the business of beauty / Tabatha Coffey with Richard Buskin.— 1st ed.
    p. cm.
  ISBN 978-0-06-202310-0
  1. Coffey, Tabatha, 1969– 2. Television personalities—United
States—Biography. I. Buskin, Richard. II. Title.
  PN1992.4.C645A3 2011
  791.430'28092—dc22
  [B]
                                          2010043035

ISBN 978-0-06-210395-6 (pbk.)

12 13 14 15 16 OV/BVG 10 9 8 7 6 5 4 3 2 1

I dedicate this book

TO MY MOTHER

I thank you for teaching me how to be

a strong independent woman.

Your love, courage, fearlessness,

and unwavering belief in me means the world.

I love you.

CONTENTS

It's Not Really About the Hair

INTRODUCTION
The Inner Bitch

FROM THE VERY START, my life was unconventional. I mean, how else would you describe a childhood spent in the strip clubs that my parents ran in Adelaide, Australia, finding friendship and a sense of normality in the offbeat company of flamboyant drag queens?

The kids at school ridiculed me for being different, and I *was* different—I didn't think like them, I didn't act like them, and being the fat kid, I also didn't look like them. What's more, I actually viewed being different as a positive attribute more than a problem. If I was a round peg and the hole was square, well, then others would need to change the hole to accommodate me, because I sure as hell wasn't going to accommodate them.

Although my life in the clubs was full of fantasy and glamour, it was also punctuated by Dad's alcohol-fueled mood swings, and was completely turned upside down when he suddenly disappeared and left my family with no money. Watching my mother pick up the pieces and keep us going taught me that in order to survive, you must take responsibility for your own actions and never trust anyone more than you trust yourself. That's why at a really young age I focused on my own passion and pursued a career as a hairdresser. Following the lead of the transvestite performers in my parents' clubs, I wanted to create looks that expressed how people felt inside rather than how others perceived them or wanted them to be. Authenticity is—and always has been—the key to who I am and who I want to include in my life.

Making my way up the industry ladder required plenty of determination and hard work, and by the time I launched my own salon, I knew how to make tough choices that weren't always popular with everyone else. Driven to be the best hairstylist and businesswoman that I could be, I always made it a point to say what I needed to say in order to accomplish what I needed to accomplish. Anyone who has worked with me knows that I don't suffer fools easily and that I won't hesitate to speak my mind. The irony of people's reaction to my candor is that I just say what most people want to say but don't have the balls to say. I tell the *truth*.

If, along the way, I've been called a bitch for being honest, I haven't taken this personally. I developed a thick skin very early in life. Being raised in strip clubs made me comfortable with who I am and open to the choices that other people make for themselves. So when television viewers who saw me on Bravo's *Shear Genius* or on *Tabatha's Salon Takeover* called me a bitch for my forthright manner, I had to find a way to incorporate this perception into a further understanding of myself. I have always strived to be myself in front of the cameras and to be honest about what I thought of other people. As a result, bloggers made assertions such as "Tabatha's an amazing stylist but a total bitch," or "She's a great hairdresser even though she's really ugly."

I suppose it's easy to call someone ugly and hit below the belt when you can hide behind a computer screen all day, or when anonymously outdoing other bloggers' venomous remarks is your vocation. I bet none of those bloggers would have had the balls to actually spout their nonsense to my face, especially since their chatter was based on nothing. If they could recognize my talent, why did it *matter* how I looked? No matter what I say, I say it to your face. If that makes me a bitch, so be it.

But, what was I supposed to do? Sit at home and wallow in self-pity while eating chocolate bars? Not bloody likely. Having never let anyone else define me before, I wasn't about to start now, and I certainly wasn't going to obsess over the insults of a few self-appointed critics. Instead of giving their bullshit comments any validity, I dusted myself off and decided to take back the word "bitch." Why should a bunch of damned bloggers get to define me as a bitch? I decided to define myself. So I reclaimed the word "BITCH" as someone who is Brave, Intelligent, Tenacious, Creative, and Honest. And because I am all of these things, I now proudly own the title . . .

Bravery—Mine is derived from being a risk taker, personally and professionally, and from always being willing to face my demons head-on.

Intelligence—I'm no idiot. Despite having left school early to pursue my career, I'm well read, well traveled, street savvy, and I'm a successful businesswoman with a strong gut instinct. What's more, unlike many women who don't want to appear intimidating, I never downplay my intelligence. I believe women can be both smart and beautiful.

Tenacity—If I'm really passionate about something, I never give up. I'm like a pit bull with a bone. I have always battled for what I want and what I believe in, and if I have to dig deeper for the energy to keep going, then that's what I do to achieve my goals.

Creativity—If I didn't have this quality, I certainly wouldn't be writing this book! I thoroughly enjoy expressing my creativity in all aspects of life, whether I'm experimenting with a new haircut, sporting a new couture outfit, or adapting to a new challenge. Creativity keeps *me* engaged and makes my life that much more interesting while I am coping with whatever comes my way.

Honesty—I think I've already covered that, haven't I? It is the key trait that makes people perceive a woman as a bitch—it intimidates people and rubs them the wrong way. Although this reaction is often due to sexism, women are more than capable of being intimidated, too. For me, honesty is saying what I think to the people around me, but it's also about being honest with *myself.* If I can't do that, then I can't be honest with *anyone.*

The more I thought about my own positive spin on the term "bitch," the more I realized that, on some level, everyone would like to be a little braver, or exercise a little more intelligence, or be a little more creative, or tenacious or honest. The truth is, all of us, women *and* men, have an inner bitch. We just have to choose how much of it to let out and when.

As soon as I embraced my own inner bitch, I felt more comfortable with myself. Owning it actually made me feel empowered, and that's what this book is about: self-empowerment and how it's all right to be who you are, stand up for what you believe in, and do what makes you happy without being defined by other people.

Tabatha Coffey, 2011

1

The Naked Truth

I GREW UP IN strip clubs, which ironically are among the most authentic and accepting places I have ever been.

You see, Mum had three sons from a previous marriage: Geoffrey, who's seventeen years older than me; Gary, who's fifteen years my senior; and Greig, who is eight years older. Gary was the only one of my brothers who ever lived near us in Adelaide, the coastal state capital of South Australia. And while he'd visit for Sunday dinners, pretty much the rest of my family—and social—life from the time I was six years old consisted of going to the trio of strip clubs that my parents ran in Adelaide's central business district and, of course, going to school.

Jeremiah's, which was the only club in town open during the day, and the only one with a proper kitchen and chef, offered businessmen a white tablecloth setting along with a prix fixe meal while they watched the girls. Housing a full bar in addition to its stage and catwalk, the place looked more like a dinner theater than a strip joint. The same air of ersatz respectability permeated both of my parents' other clubs, La Belle and Crazy Horse, where socially acceptable patrons eyed the action while seated comfortably around tables and in booths.

Forget any notion of these clubs being sleazy dives with members of the dirty raincoat brigade jerking off in the corner—cover charges and full-time security ensured that no one who walked through those doors was a slimeball, drunk, or badly behaved individual . . . although some of them may well have grown belligerent once they realized that most of the performers—and certainly the attractive ones—were transgender.

That's right, men performing as women—in those days, they were called transvestites, and to my six-year-old eyes some of those transvestites were the most beautiful women I had ever seen. Even without a stitch of clothing, they were totally convincing. While a lot of them had already undergone sex changes, the ones who still had their wedding tackle were adept at tucking their balls into their abdomens and taping their penises into their arses and concealing it all with mascara.

Unlike go-go bars, where girls dance around poles and have dollar bills stuffed into their panties, my parents' clubs featured strippers who executed fully choreographed routines—I grew up living *La Cage aux Folles*. Accordingly, during the course of two or three songs, they'd peel and shimmy their way out of incredible costumes—ranging from full-on evening gowns to spiced-up schoolgirl outfits—until they were stark naked. It was real entertainment. And many of the performers were absolute characters.

One of them, "Ingrid," had that whole Swedish thing going on, including naturally long, straight, platinum-blond hair. And before you ever heard her Aussie accent, you'd swear she just might say, "I'm feelin' *gewd*, how err *yooo*?" Ultraslim with superfine features, she was over six feet tall and had these monstrous legs that seemed to go on for miles. Ingrid may well have been my first "crush"—she was gorgeous, and onstage, wearing hairpieces that made her tresses look big and fabulous, she was a true Nordic Amazon . . . even though Mum had actually paid for her to undergo a sex change in Egypt.

Surgical advances and cultural changes have made post-op life somewhat easier today for girls like Ingrid who, back then in that chauvinistic Australian setting, had to work hard and endure plenty of heartache just to outwardly be their inner selves. Whether they were applying makeup to cover a five o'clock shadow or fearing what their straight boyfriends might do if they ever discovered that they were dating former men, those girls traveled a tough road. I remember even at a young age hearing about attempted suicides and about those who *did* commit suicide.

Whereas Ingrid was tall and slim, "Babette" was huge and

curvaceous; a curly, dark-haired Maori with a speech impediment. One night, she freaked out because she didn't have enough tape to hide her genitals before going onstage. Mum had had enough of the dressing room drama on that particular evening and barked, "Just use some fucking superglue!" Unfortunately, Babette took her "advice." Burning like crazy after finishing her routine, she couldn't unstick what she had stuck and she called my mother in tears when she arrived home.

"I can't bloody pee, it's coming out backwards!" she cried.

"Are you an *idiot*?" Mum asked incredulously. "I wasn't *seriously* suggesting that you use superglue!"

It took several days before everything loosened up, so to speak, and afterwards Babette was never without tape in the dressing room again. Not that she was the only girl to have a total meltdown. Many of the artistes were excitable and insecure, partly because of all the hormones they were taking and partly because of the social stigma and stresses associated with their life choices. Growing up in my parents' clubs introduced me to the sacrifices one must sometimes make to live an honest and authentic life. Those "girls" were just trying to be themselves, and despite the superglue debacle, my mother was always there for them if they needed money, a place to stay, or even emotional support. She was a mother figure to them, especially when their families turned their backs or kicked them out for being "different."

Some might think Mum should have made better choices

regarding my upbringing, and talking to her now I could easily say, "Look at how you *raised me*!" However, my childhood experiences really helped make me a well-rounded, well-balanced individual, and this was thanks in large part to the broad range of people with whom I came into contact, as well as the contrasting lifestyles that instilled in me my strong sense of reality.

Certainly, I *needed* a good dose of drag queen reality, because while the strippers were doing their thing in and out of fantastic costumes, I actually had to wear a very different kind of costume. Mine was the far more sedate uniform required at the posh private Walford Church of England School for Girls that I attended in Hyde Park, close to downtown Adelaide. This uniform consisted of a blue blazer, a blue-and-grey plaid skirt, a shirt, tie, and socks up to my knees. In the summer, we wore a straw hat and in the winter we sported a felt one. Fuck, how I wanted to be one of those glamorous, over-the-top creatures in my parents' clubs when I was in that getup! I would have killed to undergo some miraculous transformation with a little makeup, a fab outfit, and a wig! Instead, I packed up my lunch box every morning and trudged to school feeling less than spectacular.

None of my teachers knew about the family business. Since Dad was a qualified accountant, that's what most of them thought he did. And those who didn't think he spent his days crunching numbers weren't about to ask so long as my parents were paying the school fees. For my part, I was never told to conceal the truth; I just knew that no one would understand. Besides which, being ostracized as the "fat kid," I didn't have friends to chat with about my offbeat lifestyle and alternative view of the world anyway.

There were times when I wished I had someone to play with, but when that *did* happen I was usually frigging bored. I had nothing in common with those kids, and ditto their mothers, who'd drive them to school in their upper-class cars du jour while dressed to the nines with perfectly coiffed hair and caked-on war paint. Their posturing at the car stand didn't make any sense to me. Full drag makeup and fancy clothes were what one put on at night to look glamorous, not what one wore for a quick drive to school—a drive that *my* mum sometimes did in her pajamas after a late night working at the club.

Those other mums were done up like a dog's dinner just to maintain appearances, and I realized this when I visited their homes and saw that half of them hit the bottle at three in the afternoon while moaning about their struggles to keep up with the Joneses. Behind closed doors they weren't totally fabulous; they were totally fucking miserable, and so were their kids, who weren't getting enough attention. Even at a young age, I was able to distinguish between what was real and what was phony, and I knew that my life was far more genuine than theirs. Then again,

I was also aware and appreciative of how hard my parents had to work to *give* me that life.

Sometimes the clubs wouldn't close until three in the morning. Yet after only a few hours' sleep, Mum would get up to make me breakfast, prepare my lunch, and drive me to school. That, to my way of thinking, was how an authentic person lived—no airs, no graces, just taking care of her responsibilities. My mum was as authentic as the strippers she employed.

And all those strippers lived as "women," not drag queens. While their onstage *glamazon* personas were an act, offstage they walked around in regular women's clothes without wigs, false lashes, or heavy makeup, living as the women they *felt* they were. This was normal to me since they were so honest about it and had such strong convictions. Thinking it was weird would have been as *ab*normal as all of those overdone mums posing at the car stand while dropping off their kids.

In many respects, the transvestites were my surrogate aunts; aunts who'd say I was their child when we visited a store together, and who would talk intimately to me—and in front of me—while sitting in their birthday suits to apply makeup inside the tiny backstage rooms at both Jeremiah's and La Belle. During the day, many of them would practice their routines and rehearse new material, and if they didn't want to go home between the lunch and evening shifts, they'd also sit in those tight, cramped little rooms to sew their costumes and bullshit about anything from sex changes and hormone treatments to the latest mascara and where to find size-twelve heels.

Listening to all this while helping the girls sort through their sequins and beads, I was eventually told, "If you're going to sit here, be useful. It's time you learned how to sew." So I did, and when I became really good at it, they'd bring me their shit to work on. Beads and feathers were everywhere as those girls laid out all of their fabulous costumes and makeup on the counter for the evening. I was as transfixed by how they put themselves together as I was captivated by their chitchat about the guys they'd screwed the night before and the ones they still wanted to get their hands on.

"He was *so huge*, I didn't know where to put it . . ."

"That bitch in the red leather was all over him like a cheap suit . . ."

"We just went home, dropped some Mandrax, and fucked our brains out . . ."

The comments would be flying thick and fast while I kept my ears open and beaded their G-strings. Even though the conversation veered wildly between the raunchy and the banal, it was just girl talk, focusing on the daily grind and goings-on of some regular Auntie Mames. Nothing was ever hidden and their authenticity about who they were and who they wanted to be—even when they were dressing in outrageous costumes and putting on makeup to create an illusion for their audiences—has informed how I've conducted my own life.

My first job doing hair was actually backstage at the clubs. Without a personal stylist of any sort, the drag queens eagerly taught me how to pin-curl, hot-roller, and comb out their wigs for them. It was an auspicious start to my long and eventful career as a hairstylist, showing me that how you make someone look on the outside has everything to do with how he or she feels on the inside. Too many people live their lives according to external or societal perceptions of who, what, and how they should be. They act phony because who they truly are doesn't please their parents, partner, friends, work colleagues . . . sometimes not even *themselves*.

Invariably honest with my clients, I'm also aware that, every time they sit in my chair, a lot of what they say about how they want to look or how they perceive themselves is based on the rubbish that other people have told them. "I want to look thinner, I want to look younger, I want to look like Jennifer Aniston." If they were just more honest with themselves and real about who they are, they probably wouldn't posture with such bullshit.

I totally understand and accept that we all have to observe certain social conventions to get through life—if I said every last thing that's on my mind, I'd probably be locked up! However, if you know who you are, stay true to your beliefs, and do what feels comfortable to you as a person, it will pay off in the image that you project and in the people you attract. Authenticity is the most attractive quality a person can have. It's great when someone's appearance is an accurate reflection of who he or she is on the inside. However, authenticity is not only about looks. In a world where some people will yes you to death and be nice to your face while talking shit behind your back, it's also about meaning what you say, saying what you mean, and being comfortable with who you are.

Posers and phonies need not apply.

How to Be a Real BITCH

• Bravery is standing up for what you believe in, even if it is unpopular; it is having the courage to trust yourself because you should know yourself better than anyone else does; and it's having the balls to change what you don't like, including yourself, or else you'll just walk around, whinging like a wuss.

• Intelligence is not just being smart. Book smarts are great and street smarts are just as valuable. But real intelligence comes from trusting yourself and listening to yourself; it is knowing when to take a risk and it is knowing when to shut the fuck up. And real intelligent people, men and women, aren't afraid to let others know that they are intelligent. Acting "dumb" to make other people feel more secure is . . . dumb. Don't do it.

• Tenacity is never giving up on yourself or your dreams; it is telling people to shove their opinions up their arse when they're trying to deter or dissuade you from what you want or need; and it is standing firm when you really believe in something. Frankly, it is being a dog with a bone. It is the dogs with bones who change the world. So forget what other people think or say.

• Creativity doesn't mean you have to be an impressionist painter or a novelist. You can bring creativity into whatever you do in your work and in your life. Creativity is a way of thinking about yourself in the world. It's not settling for the path most traveled because it is easy or obvious. Sometimes you need to think out of the box and try something no one has ever done before. You need to challenge yourself to create new ideas, new ways, and new things, regardless of what you do for a living. Bill Gates and Steve Jobs aren't "artists" in the traditional sense, but their wild creativity has changed the way we understand the world. And we should all aspire to that.

• Honesty isn't just about telling other people the truth. It's also about telling yourself the truth. Sometimes you'll feel compelled to sugarcoat things or avoid the truth when it might hurt, but that is the coward's way out. I am not saying you should be mean or say things that won't help the person or the situation. But I am a big proponent of telling it like it is even when the truth can be brutal because the truth helps people be better and it does, in fact, set you free.

Fitting the Fat Peg into the Skinny Hole

I WAS ALWAYS THE fat kid. Not a bit chunky around the edges, but *obese*, and this created all sorts of issues at school, right down to my uniform, which, as I already mentioned, was an absolute disaster. Manufactured for someone several years older than me, it would have to be drastically shortened to match my height and undergo all kinds of other alterations so that the rest of it fit. It wasn't pretty. And, I suppose, *I* wasn't either, at least in the eyes of my classmates. However, beauty is in the eye of the beholder, and I beheld myself just fine . . . while enjoying good food and a lot of it.

In terms of my diet, quantity was the issue, not quality. I didn't eat a lot of junk food, but I did eat far too much of everything else, and Mum, who was also heavy, cooked most of my meals. Whereas the other kids would get a sandwich for lunch at the school "tuck shop," I might have a generous helping of roast chicken and mashed potatoes along with a slab of homemade chocolate cake. There was little moderation, and I paid the price—usually in the swimming pool. Getting into my togs was a frigging nightmare, especially since I had to do so in front of my classmates. As I'd make my way toward the pool, some of them would snicker, "Here comes Orca." I wished I was faster on my feet so I could have bulldozed the bloody lot of them into the deep end. Asthma didn't help my sporting prowess either, and when puberty endowed me with breasts at the age of ten, I stood out from the other girls in more ways than one. The hard times weren't limited to the kids either. One time I went to the PE teacher, who was also our German instructor, and told her I wasn't feeling well and needed to sit out. She told me I was just fat and lazy and made me go back and keep pace with the other kids. After gym class, my mum had to pick me up at the curb, where I had collapsed into a full-on asthma attack.

I didn't feel stigmatized. I hated being teased, but I also didn't really care to befriend my peers, so I suppose the disdain went both ways. In fact, I didn't have any friends my age and I didn't socialize at school, which meant that I was bored most of the time and this concerned my parents. There weren't that many kids in our neighborhood, but one day I overheard Dad talking to a kid on the street in front of our house. He had stopped the kid to offer him cash to play with me. I was rather horrified, mostly because I didn't want to get stuck playing with someone my own age.

But despite the tortures of school, my parents did try to reassure me that my "puppy fat" would go away. At the clubs the girls just treated me like a smart and beautiful little person who did a fine job of setting their wigs and beading their clothes. Well aware that other, average kids didn't hang out with drag queens, I felt certain that their lives weren't nearly as interesting as mine and I judged them as harshly or perhaps more harshly than they judged me. After all, they were just boring kids and I was living a really interesting life filled with really interesting adults.

One of the many things I learned from growing up around those queens was that you have to march to the beat of your own drum and fuck anyone who doesn't like the rhythm. I would have staked my life on some of those strippers being women. But others with deeper voices and more masculine features were exposed to terrible ridicule while just trying to be themselves in the daytime world. Confronted by gay bashers who called them *pooftahs* at the gas station or grocery store, the "girls" always had a "fuck you, I'm comfortable with myself" attitude—even when, at times, they'd get the crap beaten out of them. Their "difference" sometimes put them in real danger, but they marched to their own beat anyway, and I learned to adopt this attitude when dealing with schoolkids who picked on me for being unfit or ostracized me because they thought my fat might be contagious, like a case of the "cooties."

None of the strippers ever judged me or spoke down to me.

Since I treated them the way they wanted to be treated and fully accepted them as beautiful women, they responded in kind. There was mutual empathy and understanding, and that's why I was way more comfortable around them than with a bunch of mundane kids whose idea of fun was trying to come up with lame insults. My favorite activities were more creative than that, whether I was playing beauty shop with an imaginary friend, dressing my Barbie dolls and—now here's a surprise—styling their hair, or attending ballet, tap, and Spanish dance classes. Having seen the strippers in action, my favorite activities were invariably theatrical . . . I loved a touch of drama almost as much as I loved a piece of chocolate cake.

One time, while my classmates were trying to come up with parts for a school play, I sat onstage in front of a makeup mirror and performed Judy Garland's "Born in a Trunk." To them, that was weird; to me, it made perfect sense. I loved the film *A Star Is Born* and I also loved being in the clubs, so borrowing from both seemed perfectly natural. What I *didn't* love was being around kids because I really *wasn't* one. Even as the baby of the family, I lived in a grown-up world, and the rejection by my peers simply confirmed that I was different. It didn't bother me. Quite the reverse. In fact, I was more than happy to be nothing like them and started working harder to differentiate myself from them by acting and dressing differently.

For their part, my parents always perceived me as different because I was an original, independent thinker. For example, we had religious education at my primary school, and when I was seven a teacher threw me out of class for asking, "How did Mary have Jesus if she was still a virgin?" That was *good* different; the kind of different that made me more interesting. I mean, at five years old, when most other girls my age were dreaming of a princess dress, I was telling Mum that if I ever got married, I'd wear a strapless black lace wedding gown with a fishtail—clearly, those queens were *very* influential.

Just a few years later, I spotted a copy of French *Vogue* at the newsstand and begged Dad to buy it for me. It was a huge, incredibly expensive magazine and I couldn't understand a word that was printed in it, but the glossy cover was amazing, and as I flipped through it I was immediately enamored of the glamour. I reveled in the pictures of beautiful clothes, beautiful hairstyles, and beautiful makeup adorning the equally beautiful people. I wanted to live inside that magazine and I vowed that someday I would.

Thanks to the self-confidence instilled in me by my drag queen aunties, I came to realize that if I *am* different and I *am* unusual, that's a good thing. Many people are apprehensive about change and scared of being different, but I've yet to find one global definition of what it means to be "normal." In fact, we're *all* different, so I don't know what "normal" is, and what's more, I actually like to undermine people's ideas of "normal." That can be very liberating.

As a teenager, faced with the ridicule of my cruel insecure peers, I decided to embrace being different by wearing unusual, fabulous clothes, putting unique outfits together, doing crazy things to my hair, and generally being my own person. *That's* what I did to feel comfortable with myself instead of trying to lose weight in order to "fit in." As far as I was concerned, *fuck* fitting in!

Accustomed to people staring at me because I was fat, I didn't think it was odd for them to do the same when I walked down the street with writing all over my face because that, for me, was the cool new look. I thought it was brilliant—"*Here's* something for you to bloody look at!" And when all the staring started to get old, I was eager to find a place like the clubs where people embraced differences. When I was eighteen, I took a brief hairdressing course in London and was delighted to discover people who were refreshingly different and totally into it, too. After returning to Australia, I couldn't get the bug out of my arse about the English capital, so I decided to move there and have an adventure.

I loved the challenge of trying to succeed in another country, and I also acquired a taste for travel thanks to my quest for all things unique and exciting. Of course, the English enjoyed giving me a hard time when they first heard my accent, calling me "the Convict" in reference to the more than 165,000 prisoners whom the British had transported to the Australian penal colonies during the late nineteenth and twentieth centuries. However, I had no problem with the ribbing because Australians have one of the brashest senses of humor out there. We make fun of everybody, including ourselves, so when I was told that I'd come home to the "motherland," I always took it with a grain of salt. The piss-talking wasn't being done in a malicious way and I loved the people I was meeting in my new city.

The extreme ways in which Londoners crafted their looks inspired and influenced me. I loved to ride around on the double-deckers and just people-watch. The punks mixed in with the trendy girls as well as with the Sloane Rangers. And the English had such an amazing way of not taking any frigging notice of anybody around them. It really didn't matter what I looked like; no one judged me no matter how crazy I appeared, and I never felt like I stood out, at least not in a bad way. I loved that. I was experimental with my clothes and especially with my hair, but no one so much as batted an eyelid. Still chubby, I lost any self-consciousness about this because I was expressing myself so freely and I was finally around really amazing hairdressers who were inspiring me in my profession.

Working for Vidal Sassoon and then Toni & Guy, I got the training that other stylists in Australia always talked about but were too scared to pursue. And when I was hairdressing, I wasn't the fat kid or the outsider; I was a rock star, and I liked being a rock star. Not that it was always easy. When I was the head colorist at one of Toni & Guy's salons, coworkers still took digs at me for being fat. My response was always, "I may be fat, but I am really good at what I do." And frankly, they were taking the cheap shot because they knew how good I was and they wanted my position.

I'm not romanticizing my time in London. It was tough on many levels. I was making very little money and I lived in a shit-hole apartment in Kensington. The weather was freezing cold, and I had to put 50p into a slot to keep the heat on and the water hot. When I ran out of money, I'd quite literally be left out in the cold. What's more, I didn't know some of the English regimens, such as *queueing*, and when I cut in front of somebody they had no problem telling me, "Get to the back of the line, you *fat cow*!"

"Fuck off!" I'd respond. "I may be fat, but at least I'm not *ugly*!" That was the beauty of London. You could always say your piece.

Most Londoners had an "anything goes" attitude, just like in my parents' clubs. Whether you wanted to shave your head in public or stand in the middle of the street to speak your mind, they'd just roll their eyes and keep walking. Eccentricity was so much a part of the social fabric that no one even perceived it as un-usual—others with less open minds might have condemned the geeks, gays, cross-dressers, you name it, but not in London.

Another thing that made me feel right at home was the stiff upper lip that even the younger generation of English possessed. If something needed to be done, they got on with it, and that suited me down to the ground. Sure, they might whinge and bitch about something for a few seconds, but it didn't mean a whole lot because they'd still end up doing what had to be done. They weren't namby-pamby. And when shit fell apart, they'd conform to the old English joke "Let's have a cup of tea and everything will be fine." That's exactly my attitude—if you have a bad minute, sit down, have a cup of tea, regroup, and then move forward to make it right.

That's one of the reasons why I wasn't one to wallow in my weight or in being the fat kid at school. I ate what I wanted and did what I wanted, and I didn't give a shit about what the other kids called me. But when I was really fat, I have to admit that I was also lazy and didn't bother to push away from the table or exercise, even though I knew I could shed some of the weight and probably be more "popular." I didn't want to be popular and so I had no motivation. It was always a case of "Monday, I'll do it," and when Monday came I would then think, "Oh, fuck, I forgot. I'll do it next Monday . . ." I was never serious about exercising, and whenever I made the effort to diet, it wouldn't last longer than a couple of weeks. I'd miss my chips or going out to dinner with friends. Never mind the insults; it was more important to be who I felt I was and to eat what I wanted at the time.

I lacked self-discipline then, and it wasn't until I grew older that self-discipline became an important part of who I am, too. I really started exercising when I came to America. At first it was for all the wrong reasons. I wanted to belong and make friends. But as I became thinner and fitter, I found that I liked who I was more and more. I was working with a personal trainer who really pushed me and didn't let me get away with any bullshit. No more excuses like "Oh I forgot." I didn't want to let him down or disappoint him, so I kept at it and became really healthy in the process. I took the thing I hated and turned it into my friend. Eventually, I even got certified to be a personal trainer myself. Exercise turned into something I loved and craved, and I was a different person when I did it—not just on the outside but on the inside, too. The thing about being yourself is that your self is always evolving, and this will often surprise you.

For me, being comfortable with myself is not only about how I look. It's also about living honestly as who I am, even if that's different from everyone else around me. And it's about allowing myself to change and discover new versions of me: the fat me, the thin me, the Australian me, the London me, the hairdresser me. If I've pissed someone off, it's only because I'm standing up for myself and my definition of "normal." And if people have a problem with my appearance, my beliefs, or my very being, they can fuck off. Either take me how I am or forget it, because I'm going to continue to march to my own drum, *whatever* that may be.

Following Your Own Personal Style

• The problem with me giving "pointers" about following your own personal sense of style is that it's YOUR sense of style. And that is the pointer. You can read everything from French *Vogue* to celebrity rags for the latest hot trends to wear. But you need to find ways to make those looks your own. They should reflect what's inside of you— your passions, your energy, and your taste. Not everyone looks like Agyness Deyn or Lauren Conrad and you don't need to look like them to be stylish. In fact, trying to fit into those unattainable molds is the biggest mistake you can make. So look in a real mirror and ask yourself what you like, what makes you feel good about yourself, and what makes you happy. When you answer those questions, you have found your own personal sense of style. For me, the answer was simple: black.

3

The Mob and My Moral Compass

I HAVE BIG BALLS. I got them from my mum. In fact, my dad was quite the pussy. The truth is, having big balls is about standing up for what you believe in, and you don't always know what you believe in until you are faced with several directions. That's when you form your moral compass.

During my childhood, Abe Saffron was Australia's biggest mobster, and he was involved in everything from drugs, gambling, bootleg liquor, arson, and stolen goods to bribery, blackmail, extortion, prostitution, the suspicious disappearance of a moral crusader . . . and my parents' strip clubs. Not exactly the right direction for a kid, but Mum and Dad found themselves in business with the man.

Nicknamed "Mr. Sin" and "the Boss of the Cross" in reference to the brothels, bars, strip joints, and various other operations that he ran in the Kings Cross red-light district of Sydney, Abe had so many police and politicians on the payroll that, over the course of sixty years, his only major conviction was for tax evasion. He was Australia's very own Al Capone, and my parents first made his acquaintance when they lived in Sydney before I was born. That's where a lot of the drag clubs were, and among the most prominent was Abe's establishment Les Girls, located at the corner of Darlinghurst Road and Roslyn Street, in the heart of the Cross. The star attraction there was Carlotta, a transsexual showgirl who became one of the inspirations for the movie *Priscilla, Queen of the Desert*, and my parents owned a nearby coffee shop where Carlotta and a lot of the other strippers would change into their costumes.

Back then the law allowed the cops to arrest anyone who was walking around in drag, so the performers from Les Girls and other local clubs would visit my parents' coffee shop to get dressed, do their makeup, and style their wigs before rushing around the corner to go onstage. Mum and Dad were fine with that. Because all of these girls worked for Abe in the clubs, he walked into the coffee shop one day, and that was that—my parents were in business with a mobster. But that wasn't *really* that, was it? I mean, how many six-year-olds can say, "Mummy and Daddy work with a mobster." Not that I really knew what that meant. To me, he was just "Uncle Abe."

A short, fairly nondescript man, Abe Saffron, to me, looked

more like somebody's grandfather than a leading member of what has been jokingly referred to as the "Kosher Nostra." Abe was old-school. Smartly dressed without being flashy, he had little interest in calling attention to himself unless someone wasn't paying attention to his demands. Although I do remember his diamond pinky ring because most of the time he'd just walk around with his head slightly bowed, rubbing his hands together as if he was deep in thought . . . or getting ready for action. And by "action," I don't mean anything good.

Quiet-spoken, he had an air of equally understated authority that suggested you'd better not mess with him, and even at a tender age I knew what he did and who his top boys were. Still, Abe was extremely kind to *me* on the four or five occasions that we met, including the time when a guy who'd crossed him was brought into the small office at the back of Jeremiah's kitchen, where I had a makeshift bed. I often slept in there when I was at the club during a late show, and on this particular night I saw Abe give one of his boys the order to break the guy's hand.

The burly henchman picked up a slab of wood with protruding nails—normally used to post the kitchen dockets—and was about to slam it through the hysterical victim's palm when Abe spotted me and calmly remarked, "Not in front of Tabatha. Let's take care of this in another room." Turning to me, he then said, "Hi, how are you?" and engaged me in a very pleasant conversation while the three of them—one not so willingly—relocated to a different part of the club and resumed business. Abe could be *very* thoughtful . . . But the interesting thing is, at that time I was never afraid of him. He was always kind and respectful toward me—that was part of his moral code. I was a kid, and you don't fuck with a kid.

Since he didn't show up at the clubs all that often, his visits were always an event and everyone would be on their best behavior. People were petrified of him, including my father, who would get incredibly nervous and rush around shouting "Abe's coming!" while making sure everything was being done properly. As I've said, Dad was a big pussy. He had no balls. In fact, the only time he had any sort of strength to him was when he drank and would get into fights to prove what a big man he was. We found him on the doorstep more than once covered in blood after a brawl at a local pub. Without the alcohol, he would get truly tweaked whenever Abe was on his way. My mum, on the other hand, had no fear of Abe whatsoever and no problem standing up to the man. Despite sometimes playing the old-fashioned role of housewife, making our dinner, laying out Dad's clothes, and generally pandering to his needs, she was one tough cookie and she always took care of things.

One night, after I'd slept on my makeshift bed at Jeremiah's, we returned home to discover we had been robbed and that the entire house was emptied out; the sofa, the beds, everything . . . except my bedroom. That was the one room where everything was perfectly intact. The thieves had decided not to fuck with a kid. Naturally, my parents called the police and filed an insurance claim. Then, about three weeks later, Mum received a call from Abe, telling her that in exchange for half the insurance money, she could pick up all of our furniture at the pier in Port Adelaide. "Go fuck yourself!" she responded. "I'm not getting involved!"

That's how strong Mum could be in the face of real danger. Abe was testing her to see if she'd squeal on him, and Dad was his usual terrified self, saying, "Take the stuff back. Don't annoy them." But Mum wouldn't budge. "Fuck 'em," I remember her saying. "They can dump everything in the Port River. I don't care, no one will find it." She didn't want any part of Abe's scam, but she had also proven her loyalty to him. Mum was *very* loyal, but she also didn't have a dishonest bone in her body. Well aware of who she was doing business with, Mum never adopted any of Abe's unsavory practices, and she had rules and values that she'd never betray because she had her own moral compass.

When any of Abe's "hot" merchandise found its way into the clubs, Mum told him to remove it. The cops were always buzzing around and she wasn't about to take the fall for him. "Get your bloody stuff out of here!" she would scream, and she'd stand firm even when he'd try to sway her in his calm and collected way. If Dad was there, he wouldn't say a word. Instead, he'd run and hide somewhere. Probably looking for a drink. *Pussy!* He knew Mum would handle things, and so did I. Standing five feet ten inches and boasting a powerful, authoritative voice, she could be very intimidating, and she backed this up with an iron will and strong self-confidence.

Mum hated weakness; she had no tolerance for it, even with regard to my father. What's more, she was incredibly hardworking. She couldn't stand laziness, and letting others take care of the business just wasn't an option. Then again, she wasn't about to let anyone bully her, and I don't like to be bullied either. I admired her as a kid, and I inherited my toughness from my mum . . . as well as her propensity for swearing like a truck driver to get her point across—whatever works!

But despite the swearing, Mum never had a drink, she hated all forms of drugs, and she'd never do anything that exploited children. Again, that was her moral compass. Say or think whatever you like about Mum and the environment in which she raised me, but amid all the craziness there was her compass, and I was raised to develop my own moral code, too. Let's face it, lots of kids are raised under screwed-up circumstances and are never taught to form a moral compass of their own. The well-to-do kids from my private school came from broken homes with alcoholics and other unhappy people as well. They just didn't admit to it and they certainly didn't do anything about it because they were so afraid of being judged for their flaws that they tried to hide themselves from sight rather than develop themselves. Even wholesome family entertainment like *Bambi* spun me for more of a loop than Abe Saffron's goon breaking someone's hand. I mean, what is the message of death and carnage in that "kids" cartoon? Bambi and his mother go off in search of grass to eat and his mother gets shot and killed. Then, when Bambi tries to mate, he has to fight off a violent suitor and kill him to get the doe-fawn. And finally, saving his love from a fire, Bambi is shot and narrowly escapes with his father. When my mum took me to the drive-in to see the film, I bawled like a baby, and her response was "What kind of violent fucking bullshit is this?" I told you Mum likes to swear.

While Abe Saffron was undoubtedly a debauched character in many ways, he showed me that he could also be very kind. Yes, there were the criminal activities and thuggish behavior, but the manner in which he treated me showed that he, too, had values that he wouldn't breach. And although I'm in no way condoning the conduct that once led Senator Don Chipp to stand up in Australia's Federal Parliament and describe Abe as "one of the most notorious, despicable human beings—if one can use that term loosely—living in this country," I do think he lived by a code. If someone crossed him, his code allowed him to seek retribution but only in line with that code.

I'm not saying I agree with the mobster mentality. But as all good Martin Scorsese movies demonstrate, even the Mob maintains a code of conduct, and when you breach it, those guys let you know it in no uncertain terms. Similarly, when you breach *my* moral code, I will let you know it in no uncertain terms. No, I don't whack people, but I am very honest and I'm very strong in holding to my beliefs. I have *big balls*. Just like my mother.

The criteria that people use to judge others are often ridiculous—"She's a stripper, so she's a bad person." Just because someone's a go-go dancer doesn't mean she's devoid of a moral compass, and you don't have to be a teetotaling Bible-thumper to have strong beliefs. Examples of a moral compass can come from many places—even Abe Saffron. And a good moral compass doesn't need to condemn other people for who they are.

From Mum I learned not only to stand up for myself, but also to stand up for my convictions. That's why, in the face of naysayers, I've never backed down. If I believe in something, I'll follow it through to the end, whether this entails confronting someone or simply not giving up. It's not always about me getting in somebody's face; it's also about sticking to my guns when someone decides he or she is right and I am wrong. It's just like when the kids in school judged me for being fat or when Ronno in *Bambi* tries to force Faline to go with him or when any other bully tries to mess with the underdog—I become a pit bull with a bone. I can't let go. I'll always root for the underdog.

People often won't do that because they don't like confrontation or they're afraid they will be labeled a bitch. *No*, that's just standing up for yourself. Of course, doing this can sometimes land you in even deeper shit, but I don't think about that at the time if I believe in something strongly enough. I do actually have a three-second rule—when I want to make a point, I've got to think for three seconds before I let it out. That way, in the heat of the moment I won't say something that I'll totally regret. A three-second rule is a good way to remain within the boundaries of your own moral compass. Check yourself by asking, "Is that what I really mean, what I really want, what I really believe in?" If the answers are yes, then say it and don't back down.

I'm not a pussy when it comes to saying what I think. I'm comfortable looking at situations from other people's points of view because I want to understand where they are coming from and I'm confident in my *own* point of view. People who refuse to empathize are simply insecure and feel vulnerable when faced with the possibility that the other person is actually right. Again, if you have a strong moral compass, this is never an issue. You can be wrong and still be a good person—it's *okay* to be wrong. And admitting it is a sign of strength.

By no stretch of the imagination am I right all of the time, and I'm totally open to learning from how other people do things. But when I truly believe in something, it's not about believing I'm right; I just know this is the right thing for *me* and my moral code, and that if I go with someone else's point of view or demands, it's not going to work for me. In that sort of situation, I don't care if you offer me money—there have been big deals that I've turned down because they haven't felt comfortable to me. They're against what I believe. Like my mother, I'm not interested in exploiting kids or taking advantage of women in need. I'll stand by what I believe in and wait for the right reward.

So *what* if standing up for myself and what I believe in means I'll be perceived as a bitch? I've already reclaimed that word according to my own moral compass: bravery, integrity, tenacity, creativity, and honesty. In fact, come to think of it, being a bitch *IS* my moral compass. And following it ensures that I won't do anything that makes me feel like a fraud and a phony. That way, if people *do* think I'm a bitch, then I'm a bitch who sleeps really well at night. And this book is about helping you to sleep well, too.

The Three-Second Rule

- Heat-of-the-moment words can often burn you in the end. So I have a three-second rule, which is quite simple and can be applied in any situation. I've been there, trust me. Someone pisses you off or crosses you in some way and you immediately have the perfect comeback or tell-off. But you need to count to three before you say it. Just to check yourself and make sure what you want to say is what you really want to say. I think of it like having a cop in my head so I can police myself and know when not to say certain things. Those three seconds may feel like a lifetime when you're in the moment, but they give you just enough time to process what you are saying and whether you should say it. So you can always say what you mean and mean what you say—no apologies later and no unintended consequences. Counting to three has saved me from major escalations with surly traffic cops and ridiculous salon owners alike. It's as easy as counting one, two, three.

4

I
Will
Survive

MY FATHER WAS A bit of a Dr. Jekyll and Mr. Hyde. Or rather, a Dr. Jekyll and Mr. Drunk. And when he was drinking you didn't want any part of his world, which was difficult because while Mum was busy running the clubs, it was Dad who took me swimming, and bought me ice cream, and generally took care of me. I could play with him, talk with him, ask for his help, and even cry on his shoulder . . . so long as he wasn't sloshed.

He'd frequently have bouts of intense drinking. Sometimes he'd go on benders that would last for several days, and I could immediately tell when trouble was brewing. More diminutive in stature than my mother, he was usually a very personable, jovial, impeccably dressed guy. He'd take a change of clothes to work in case it was hot, and then, when he returned home, slip out of his perfectly crisp, tailored shirt, have a shower, and put on a smoking jacket and cravat. Weird but true. He cared about how he looked and how he presented himself, but that persona would disappear after one beer too many or whatever the drink of choice might have been. And in a flash you'd realize he wasn't who you thought he was.

His posture would change, the look on his face would change, the tone of his voice would change—*everything* would change as his impeccable stance began to crumble and it became clear how trashed he really was. The look in his eyes would actually transition from that of an affable person who liked a good conversation to that of someone who was evil, and although he never hit Mum or me, he could be pretty violent. For example, he set a women's hair on fire at a pub once. I don't mean, "Oops, my lighter slipped, I'm so sorry." I mean, "Fuck you!" and he sent her up in flames on purpose. On another occasion, he hit a fellow pub goer in the face with a mug. These were the Mr. Hyde moments.

My father would spin on a dime. As soon as a beer or Scotch tipped him over the edge, he'd go off his head and smash the house, putting his fist through walls and doors or throwing furniture out the window. Mum didn't take crap from anyone, but she was scared when Dad was drunk. She left her first husband, my brothers' dad, after he had been physically violent toward her, and she never really knew what Dad might do when he was completely shit-faced. If we were lucky, he'd pass out. That was the best-case scenario. The worst was that he'd just lose his mind, and this could be over virtually nothing. But while she didn't want to antagonize him if he went into one of his booze-fueled rants, she also didn't cower. When he screamed, she'd hold her ground and fire straight back. And that made for what one might call a volatile home life.

One time, when Mum told him "I think you've had enough beer, you should go to bed," Dad made it clear he wanted another bottle by picking up a La-Z-Boy chair and chucking it through a window. Although not tall like Mum and my brothers, he was a strong man, so there was no telling what he might destroy when he crossed over to the dark side, let alone who he'd pick on.

I knew when it was time to go, and Mum knew when it was time to get me away from him. She always had a change of clothes in the car, and I had a school uniform in there just in case we needed to spend the night at a friend's house because Daddy Dearest was in one of his moods. I remember an incident when I was twelve: he was drunk, and after Mum found him staggering down the street from a pub, she tried to cajole him to get into the car. Of course, he became abusive, so she tried to play the child card, telling him, "Get in for your *daughter's* sake." He responded by calling me a cunt and kept walking.

My father didn't actually lash out at me very much. Still, I knew when to hide and my mother wouldn't leave me with him if he was drinking. The only time she did was when I was a toddler. He paid less attention to me than to the bottle and I ended up in the hospital after eating a box of matches. Mum never made that mistake again.

From a young age, I could see my father's loss of control when he drank, and I knew I never wanted to be like that. Self-control has always been a priority, and while I'm not going to say there haven't been nights when I've drunk too much, acted a bit of a fool, and had a hell of a headache the next morning, booze has never been an issue for me. Ditto Mum, who never drank and never needed to. I can remember just one occasion when she had a couple of drinks, and she was immediately red-faced and tipsy.

That's why there was a split in our house. My father clearly needed to drink, and this need increased to the point where Mum actually tried to curb it with pills that were prescribed by a doctor friend. Dad didn't realize she was sneaking the pills into the vitamin regime that he took every morning, but she sure as hell knew when he'd been imbibing because just one nip would give him stomach pains, make him nauseous, and turn his ears bright red. It was hilarious to watch him try to figure out why he couldn't get past that first drink.

I never quite knew what my father's demons were, but without a shadow of a doubt he was fighting *something*. When the alcohol kicked in, it was as if he turned into the devil, and the next day he'd invariably be sorry—the archetypal dog with his tail between his legs. Acting all nicey-nice, he'd try to be the good husband and father by abstaining from drink, taking us to a fancy restaurant, or splashing out on gifts and flowers. But none of that worked on me because it was too late. I already knew I couldn't trust him. He was my father but he was also a monster. Sad but true.

And the gifts weren't all that innocent, as it turned out. Whether or not he'd been drinking, he always bought us flowers on Friday. It was a thoughtful treat . . . until Mum went to collect him from work one day and discovered he was fucking the florist. A year earlier, when I was ten, my parents had closed the strip clubs and opened a sex shop on Flinders Street, in Adelaide's central business district, where they sold books, toys, videos, and other paraphernalia. Not only did they want to dissolve the roller-coaster partnership with Abe Saffron, but the club hours were crazy and they knew they could make good money more easily with one of the city's first adult stores. My parents were entrepreneurs for sure.

The place was called Ecstasy, and this turned out to be pretty bloody appropriate that afternoon. Assuming that Daddy had gone out to get a newspaper because the door to the store was locked, Mum let herself in and found him fooling around with the flower lady. I was sitting in the car, and I remember her coming out, giving me five bucks to buy myself a milk shake, and telling me she was going to be a while because she'd just caught him with another woman. As usual, *nothing* was kept from me.

While I sat in the car, drank my milk shake, and listened to the radio—as one does on such occasions—Mum confronted her husband and kicked out his lover. Then we drove home without him. Mum was pretty angry and she certainly knew some people who had less than savory jobs, so she hired someone to make her point for her. The next day the bloke drove a truck through the front window of the girl's nursery. No one was hurt but my mother felt a hell of a lot better.

But the fact of the matter was Dad was not going to give up the girl, so Mum came up with a truly stunning arrangement: one week, Daddy would spend four days with his bit on the side and three days with us; then, the following week, he'd spend three days with her and four with us, continuing this schedule on a rotating basis. It was bizarre to me because my parents still shared the same bed—God only knows what was going on between them. And I soon began to wish that Dad would just leave.

My father didn't act crazy when he was home—he was on quite good behavior—but I kept thinking our lives would be so much easier if he wasn't around. Not only did I know his affair was wrong, but I could also see what it was doing to my mother. Things were really awkward and uncomfortable when he walked in the door. I mean, we could hardly sit down and say, "So, what have you been up to for the past three days?" or "What did *you* do last night?" I was more tempted to ask, "If you don't want to be here, why don't you *fucking go*?" Clearly, he was not invested in my mother or me.

To me, the whole setup didn't make any sense, but it continued for several months until Mum finally said, "Enough." She understandably bore a lot of hostility toward the cow who was servicing her husband, and matters came to a head one night when, after having dinner with my brother Gary, we returned home to find Daddy lying in bed, covered in blood, wearing a suit that was totally shredded. Of course, he was drunk, and he'd apparently jumped out of the florist's car while she was driving down the highway. She had given him an ultimatum: him and her or him and us, and he made his decision by leaping from her speeding vehicle and landing on our doorstep. Quite the fucking bargain . . .

Dad behaved himself during the next couple of months, even though he kept saying the store wasn't doing so well and money was tight. This was strange for me because I had always been able to have anything I wanted and this was the only time when Mum would tell me she had to check with my father before we bought something. But aside from the pocketbook, family life appeared to be bubbling along until we all returned from spending the weekend with my grandmother in Melbourne, which was about a ten-hour drive away. The next morning, I went to school, Daddy went to work, and when Mum collected me she said, "We're going to pick up your father, who's tired from the trip and wants an early dinner. He called to ask what we're having and I told him we're having roast chicken."

When we arrived at the shop, the door was locked, and Mum said, "Oh, he must have gone to get a paper. I'll collect his things . . ." Talk about déjà vu all over again! The only difference was instead of catching my father with the florist, she found a suicide note, five dollars, and his wedding ring.

During the strip club days, Mum had befriended the local police and paid them to keep things running smoothly. So she called a couple of the sergeants to try to locate Dad because she knew damn well he hadn't killed himself. So did I. My father had no balls, as I have said before. And I knew there was no way he could have done anything that involved inflicting pain on himself. He may have been a drunk who would leap from a speeding car, but he was definitely not suicidal. The guy was a total fucking pussy. And he was also a bloody crook. When Mum went to the bank the next day, she discovered that during the time he'd returned to live with us, her "better half" had been methodically siphoning their joint account and had left us with nothing.

While my mother may have ruled the business with an iron fist, my father was an accountant by trade and he had always been the one to do the banking and pay the bills. The result was that after years of slogging her guts out, treating him like Little Lord Fauntleroy, and putting up with his drunken shit, Mum now had just five bucks and me. Despite being broke, I was relieved about the situation. No more drunken binges and crazy nights driving around in the car with my school uniform in hand. My mother, however, wanted to know where the fuck her husband had gone with all our money. And if anyone could have found him, it was her—she certainly had the connections—but he had disappeared into thin air. Even the police, with the help of Abe Saffron, couldn't find him, and that was saying something. But instead of wallowing in anger, she went into survival mode. And no matter how hard it would be to start over on five dollars, I knew she would be able to take care of me and move on with our lives. You see, my mum is a survivor. No matter what life throws at her, she comes up swinging—or hiring someone to drive a truck through your window. And that is exactly how she raised me. I will survive.

Once we regrouped, Mum tried to run the sex shop on her own. But she quickly realized it was hard to do that while taking care of me and even harder to pay my posh private school's astronomical fees. So, within a few months Ecstasy was closed, and with my father nowhere to be found and her own mother in failing health, she moved us to Melbourne.

We initially lived with my grandmother so Mum could care for her while we started over. I attended a public school and

Mum worked as a restaurant manager to make some money. At least that job was similar to what she'd done at the clubs, and it also provided her with a little more flexibility to look after me. She had gone from being a business owner and boss to the hired help slogging in a greasy spoon, but she did it with grace and with an intense work ethic. And I carry that with me even today. No matter how life sets you back on your heels, you have to come back with poise and drive. I remember meeting a minister once who when asked, "How are you?" would reply, "Quite gracious, thank you." And grace is all you need.

My older brothers Geoffrey and Greig lived in Melbourne, and so did some of the strip club drag queens from Adelaide who had relocated there, so Mum and I had a solid network of familiar faces, friends and family. Since Melbourne was definitely a lot more cosmopolitan and sophisticated than Adelaide, the move was exciting for me. Sure, there were times when I'd think about Dad, but I was still too young to get really pissed off at him. That would come later, when I hit my teens and was able to fully comprehend what an asshole he was. This is when I also started to understand the difference between being a bitch and being an asshole—and I don't make the distinction tongue in cheek. A bitch is someone who is self-possessed and will take care of herself. She is not looking to hurt anyone and is, in fact, often quite empathetic and caring. An asshole is someone who doesn't give a shit about anyone else, mostly because he is quite self-destructive. I am a bitch. My father was an asshole.

Long after Mum found my father's phony suicide note and we moved to Melbourne, Gary ran into my father at a shopping mall in Adelaide, but Dad just walked right past him. Stunned, my brother followed him and noticed that he was working in a store there—amazingly, it was a *flower shop*. Gary gave Mum the details, and while she wanted no part of my father, I called the store and asked to speak with him. The silence on the other end of the phone lasted an eternity. Finally, he got on the line, and although I immediately recognized his voice, he said no one by that name worked there and hung up on me. I finally had confirmation that he wasn't dead; that I was right; that he had walked out. It was a double-edged sword. I wanted to be right, but I wanted to be wrong. I wanted him to be alive, but I wanted him dead, too. And I couldn't very well let it go.

My father didn't come from a very close family, but his father kept in distant contact with me and he'd send checks for my birthday. So I wrote Dad a letter, asking him, "How could you walk out on us in that way?" and "What kind of gutless wonder doesn't even acknowledge his own kid?" Then I sent it to my grandfather to forward to his son. My grandfather responded by sending me the phone number of Dad's lawyer, but when I called the attorney, he told me I was a very angry little girl and that he wouldn't let me speak to my father. It was surreal on every level.

About eighteen months after our move, my maternal grand-mother passed away, and Mum decided we should relocate to Surfers Paradise, a suburb of Queensland's Gold Coast that, thanks to its subtropical climate, golden beaches, canal water-front homes, and modern high-rise apartments, truly does live up to its name. I began working as a hairdresser's apprentice, found a girlfriend, and started to let go of all the resentment I had toward my father walking out . . . until I was seventeen and needed a passport to travel to London.

In those days, minors applying for a passport had to be accompanied by their parents to an interview with the local postmaster, and since my father wasn't around, Mum had to bring her divorce papers. I hadn't seen them and didn't know anything about how the event had transpired, so this was yet another cold shower. Without her knowledge, Dad had placed newspaper advertisements stating he was looking for her in or-der to file a divorce action. Mum never saw any of the ads, so, after placing them for the requisite number of months, he was able to divorce her in absentia. The papers had arrived out of the blue, but what really shocked me was that in the section where he'd been asked to list his dependents, he'd stated there were none. Zero, zilch. In other words, I didn't exist according to my "suicided" father.

When Mum showed the postmaster my birth certificate with

both of my parents' names, as well as her marriage and divorce certificates, she explained the situation and I got my passport. But the father odyssey was not over. Apparently, Australia is not as big as one would like to think. Shortly after I'd relocated to London, Mum and I returned to Adelaide to spend Christmas with my brother Gary, and while we were there we ran into an old family friend who said she'd seen Dad in a shopping mall.

Mum, my sister-in-law, and I scoured every single store in that mall, but there was no sign of him. We were convinced our friend was seeing things, mistaking hairy old codgers for my father years later. We gave up and went to have lunch in the food court . . . and there he was. As I turned around, he was standing about twenty feet away, so I pointed him out to my mother and she immediately marched me over to him and gave a speech about what a good person I had grown into and how much I'd accomplished. The entire time, Dad looked down at the ground and never said a word. Then he got up from his seat and walked away.

I couldn't fucking believe it. The coward wouldn't even look me in the eye. I told my mother, "I'll be back," and followed him to a clothing store. He was just standing there, so I walked over to him, and cornered like a rat, he managed to open his mouth and say, "You're a very lucky little girl." I was twenty-one years old, and in that moment I looked at him and thought,

"You know what, I really *am* lucky. Because you left and I didn't have to deal with your shit. It doesn't matter what I say to you, because you'll never understand. And it doesn't matter what you say to me, because it'll never change what you did. All that matters is, I survived." Ironically, it was partly because of my father that I grew up around tranny strippers who never pussied out or walked away from who they were. And in that moment I knew I didn't need my dad in order to be whole. I knew that on some level he really was dead to me. I turned around, walked out, and never saw him again.

And I knew I would never be like him either. I am incredibly responsible and I make sure I can always take care of myself and the people I love. Watching my mother relinquish far too much trust to my father taught me to take responsibility for *myself*, even if I'm in a relationship. It's okay to trust someone, but you still have to be present, which is something Mum clearly wasn't when her husband was helping himself to *their* money and running off with the florist. The number one person you need to trust is yourself. Then you know you can survive no matter what.

When a marriage falls apart, inevitably people wonder, "What the fuck am I going to do *now*?" My mum was responsible enough to realize, "I've got to pick up the pieces, make money, feed the two of us, put clothes on our backs, send my child to school, and keep some semblance of normality," and that's exactly what she did. You can't sit around and whinge and wallow in the circumstances. You have to survive. And being strong for yourself is the best way to do that. Ironically, my father's presence made my mother weak, but his disappearance made her strong. She survived. And so did I.

How to Survive a Shit Storm

- Hunker down. You have to be steady on your feet—literally and metaphorically. Batten down the hatches for the bumpy ride. If you don't, you'll blow away.

- Make sure you can rely on yourself. Dear God, if you can't rely on yourself, who can you rely on? I am talking to you: the drunks standing outside a club looking for someone to get them home, the idiot who leaves his wallet hanging out of his pocket and it's gone, all the people out there who hope someone else will look out for them or assume nothing bad will happen no matter how careless they are. Rely on yourself because that's your best hope. Am I saying never trust anyone? No. Am I saying don't ask for help? No. But in the end, you need to know you yourself are solid, good to go, and reliable.

- Know what's going on. There is nothing worse than someone who is just a hot mess, lost and wondering how they got there. You need to always keep your wits about you and have a plan. The more you don't know, the more vulnerable you are.

- If all else fails, when the shit flies, duck.

5

Fuck Flying a Flag

FUCK THE RAINBOW FLAG and the coming-out anthems and all the hoopla. I'm here, I'm queer, and I *am* going shopping.

Even being gay requires your own definition. Gay pride parades can boast diversity all they want, but every year I see the same picture on the front page of the New York newspapers. It's always a bunch of hairy bears with potbellies dressed in leather outfits dancing on a colorful float surrounded by outrageous drag queens on stilts. It's never a picture of the senior citizens group or the firefighters or any of the other boring factions. And every year, I hear the frustrated rebuttals of the more staid, mainstream, if you will, gays and lesbians who drive Volvos and invest in 401(k)s like their straight brethren. They start clamoring about how the media is always out to paint the LGBT "community" as "freaks."

Freaks or not, leather daddies and drag queens certainly have had a long, illustrious history, not only being part of the "community," but actually helping to form it during such seminal moments as the Stone Wall riots. And yet even the leather daddies and drag queens would like to keep a few groups out of said "community." During the gay pride parade on the twenty-fifth anniversary of the Stonewall riots, the group NAMBLA (the National Association for Man-Boy Love) wanted to march. Pretty much everyone in the community, including those considered to be on the fringe, wanted the group left out. People were concerned that the inclusion of such a group would reflect poorly on the community as a whole and would give the media an even more salacious picture for the front page. Let me just stop to say, man-boy love is not part of my moral compass and I am not condoning any kind of underage or illegal activity. But the tension this issue caused proves that like every other social group, the gay community is composed of people who conform and people who don't, and just as annoyingly, it is composed of people who are really vocal about whether you fit in or you don't. There are rules, and to be a "good gay" one learns the rules. But let's face it, I don't like rules or conformity. You'll never see *me* and my girlfriend walking down the street in the West Village or

West Hollywood in matching outfits. Not so much. I will march to my own drum as a gay woman, defining myself in that aspect of my life my own way, just like I do with every other personal definition. No gay pride parade needed. Not that I don't like a good parade, but I don't want the gay community to dictate who I am or who I should be any more than I want the straight world to. I'm not in this life to judge anyone else and I don't want to be judged either.

For a long time I wasn't sure about participation in any kind of "community." As far back as I can remember, despite my childhood fantasy to one day wear a strapless black lace wedding gown with a fishtail, I never really wanted to get married and I certainly never wanted to have children. I grew up having crushes on drag queens, so it's doubtful I was ever going to take the "traditional" path. However, I definitely needed to grow up and get to know myself better in order to accept who I truly am and to be ready for love.

The first time I slept with a girl was when I was sixteen. We met in a club. I was already living alone and working full-time in a hair salon. I'd always liked makeup and fashion, yet I naturally gravitated toward hair. So, when I was fifteen, Mum got me a job assisting stylists after school and on weekends. Those stylists taught me how to shampoo while rinsing out color for them and helping with the rollers. Everyone apparently liked having me around, and I really, *really* loved what I was doing, so I quit school—which I fucking hated anyway—and started my apprenticeship, attending night classes to get my high school diploma. That was the deal I made with Mum and it worked out just fine.

Mum was a doer—when I lived at home, she would do my laundry, make my dinner, and do all these things for me that, although lovely, didn't allow me to be independent and take care of myself. Having my own apartment in Surfers Paradise, about five minutes away, meant I had to pay the rent, feed myself, clean my clothes, and get my arse up when it was time to go to work. And it also meant I could spend quality time with my first girlfriend.

Growing up around mostly older people, I gravitated toward older friends and they helped get me into the clubs. The majority of those clubs were gay bars, where—probably due to my upbringing—I felt much more comfortable than in straight clubs. So, when this dark curly-haired girl approached me in a crowded bar, I thought two things: "Wow, she has great hair," and "Mmm, I'd like to kiss her." Sandy was nineteen, worked as a clothing store manager, and actually lived in the town next to mine. And while there was nothing extraordinary or heart-stopping about her, this was my first lesbian U-Haul date. We moved in together after a few months.

Even after we started dating, I never felt the need to come out by making a grand announcement to family, friends, or work colleagues—I still don't think being who you are requires an event with a Diana Ross anthem. I honestly never thought that being gay was bad. Ever since I was a kid, I had been taught to accept other people. I mean, so what if I'm gay? Being with a woman felt completely normal, so my attitude was "Fuck it. I'm good, so who cares what anyone else thinks." What surprised me was that Mum wasn't exactly of the same mind.

Because I'd been raised in a drag queen environment by a mother who'd employed those girls, nurtured them, supported them, and socialized with them, it was hardly a stretch for me to assume she'd be fine with the news that *I* was gay. I'd heard no remarks or conversations that would lead me to think otherwise. For God's sake, one of the first weddings I attended, at age nine, was a union between two lesbians. The happy couple worked as bartenders at the club, so all the girls attended and Mum seemed absolutely fine with it. Back then it wasn't legal in Australia, but the ceremony took place in a church which made it feel quite official, and it seemed perfectly normal to me. There were flowers and an organ and all the conventional trimmings. Afterward, Mum took me to the reception at the girls' house, in their backyard. So I had no reason to think she would reject my own relationship . . . *Wrong!*

Before Sandy and I moved in together, I was having dinner at Mum's house and I casually told her that I'd met someone. But when I told her *who* I was dating, she was furious: "My daughter is *not* going to be a fucking dyke!" I can't recall every word of her diatribe, but suffice it to say there were derogatory remarks about my sexuality and pissy comments that made it clear she was disgusted with the whole thing. I was really shocked and disappointed.

"Isn't it interesting?" I shot back. "While it's okay for everyone else, it *isn't* okay for your own bloody daughter!"

Mum's reaction threw me for a loop because I looked up to her. Acutely aware of how much Mum wanted me to present her with a grandchild someday, I felt bad, and our relationship became quite strained. We are both strong, uncompromising personalities, and we basically entered a yearlong standoff on the subject, which was hard to take in light of how much I respected her.

My mother is a complicated woman. Clearly. Despite raising me in a transsexual strip club and allowing me to be in the presence of one of Australia's most notorious mobsters, my mother was really quite traditional. She laid out my father's clothes every morning and she made family dinner every night. My mum hated the fact that kids teased me for being fat, and when she drove me to school each morning, she would always give me a little batch of courage (and a big lunch) to get me through the day. And when my father abandoned us, I felt rejected, which I'm sure was hard for her to deal with. To that end, I think Mum always hoped I would be able to fit in. I think she imagined that as I got older, and thinner, and more successful, life would get easier. And when I told her I was gay, all that hope was momentarily shattered. My mother didn't want to see me rejected anymore. This is not a unique story; it's far too common for gay people when we come out to our parents. But what is interesting is that a woman as uncommon as my mother could be so common in her reaction. Let's face it, her moral compass is not exactly conservative or traditional. And ultimately, her moral compass didn't include being homophobic either. But she had to work out all the cultural stereotypes and bullshit about what it "means" to be gay. She had to realize being gay didn't mean I would wind up alone, an alcoholic, on a bridge somewhere ready to jump. She had to understand that being gay was part of what made me *me* and what made me happy. Once she got that, we never really had to discuss it again. Me being gay is like me having blue eyes to her now. It's part of who her daughter is. My mother has pretty much always lived with me, and while I have been writing this book and making

Season Three of my TV show, she has been sick. My partner has been taking care of her and I won't say it has been an easy task. But Mum relies on her when I am not there and Mum knows she is her family. We aren't exactly traditional and that's totally normal to us.

Throughout that early rough patch, however, Mum's cold shoulder made me start to question myself and what was right for me. She was the only person I respected enough at that point in my life to actually make me unsure of myself, and during that year I *was* really unsure. I wanted her approval, and having witnessed the struggles of the transvestite strippers at her clubs, I decided that life would be a damned sight easier if I played by the hetero rules. I don't think I was trying to fit in so much when I chose to give the conventional route another go. I was really looking for Mum's approval. So I ended the relationship with my girlfriend. And following a couple of short-term meaningless flings with other girls, I did precisely what I'd vowed I would never do and changed who I was to meet someone else's definitions. Just two years after having come out of the closet, I dove straight back in and began dating guys again.

But trying to please my mum also meant I had to quell some of my own desires and that was *very* challenging. I started dating men who were flash-in-the-pan characters, the type who never offer a commitment—much like my runaway Dad. This was exactly what I wanted at the time, because I wasn't looking for anything serious with a guy. It was easier for me if they weren't going to stick around. I didn't want to get married. I didn't want to have children. I didn't want to settle down and feel trapped.

After I moved to America, I frequented New York City straight clubs like the Tunnel on Eleventh Avenue and the China Club on West Forty-seventh Street, and most of the door people knew me. It was a great distraction from the banal grind of doing hair in the suburbs, as well as a way for me to try to fit in with the people on this side of the pond. For a while, I even dated an NFL football player who I met in one of the clubs. But I soon realized I had enough of pretending that I enjoyed men's boring stories . . . and their boring sex. It turns out that taking the conventional route when you are unconventional doesn't actually make life any easier. You have to find yourself and be yourself if you are going to live your own life. I was young, learning my craft as a hairdresser, and ready to go out and make my mark on my own. No boyfriend need apply.

I entered a period when I just avoided dating *anyone*. I preferred to date me, which helped me get to know myself a little better. I started to realize that I couldn't change who I was, even for my mother. And I figured out that my identity wasn't built around another person. I had to build my own identity. I didn't need to date someone to define myself. Figuring that out was a big life lesson. I highly recommend self-dating; it is very therapeutic. Finally focused on my career, I wanted to be a great hairdresser, so I worked like a maniac to make that happen. There wasn't really room in my life for another person at that point. Another person would have to come later, once I figured out who I was and how to be me. Parade or no parade.

Literally and figuratively, it's hard for a lot of us to look in the mirror, but that's something I've tried to do all my life, and I actually prefer to look in my own mirror to figure out what's going on than turn away from it or see a false reflection. I've always been very good at checking in with myself, talking things through with myself, and analyzing myself. While, like everyone else, I sometimes struggle to be honest with myself, I have a hard time looking in the mirror when I do things that I'm uncomfortable with. During those times I tend to make everyone around me uncomfortable, too, even if they don't know why. When I was with women, I was me; when I was with men, I was someone else, and I was angry with myself for allowing that.

The fact is, I can be a miserable wench if I'm not allowed to be me—by other people's standards or by the cop in my own head. It doesn't matter if I'm being good, bad, or ugly—I need to be me. When I try to do or say something that pleases other people but doesn't please me, it becomes so forced that I have a really hard time dealing with myself. That's when I can easily turn into the bitch that no one, including myself, wants me to be (as opposed to the kind that I've already defined).

I am a gay woman. It is *who I am.* Like having blond hair or fair skin, it is *me.* And that is what my mother needed to understand. So I drew a line in the sand. "Fuck it, this is who I am and it's a little bit late to stop me now." Having raised a feisty kid, she realized I wasn't going to back down or compromise who I was.

"If you have that much of a problem with it, then you don't have to see me," I told her. That was it. Mum's not a fool, she wasn't going to lose a daughter over our disagreement, and while it took some time for her to warm up to the idea, she didn't disown me or stop speaking to me. It was a long rocky road, but ultimately, I was lucky because even though mothers are supposed to accept their kids, as many gays and lesbians know, it doesn't always work out that way.

Ironically, I have now come full circle on the marriage thing, as well. When I was young, I thought getting married and having kids was for other people. And let's face it, my parents didn't exactly provide me with the best example of mar-

riage. I wanted to travel the world and do hair and be fabulous
and date beautiful women. And I have done all of those things
and then some. More recently, however, my priorities have
shifted. Call it age, call it being in love, call it whatever you
want, people change. So I have become involved in California's
marriage equality campaign, doing public speaking engage-
ments and other PR work to try to make sure that gays and
lesbians have the right to get married. Whether or not I personally want to make that kind of commitment is *my* choice,
not my neighbors', and it is shocking to me that a legal right
can still be withheld from an entire group of people. So I have
also come to realize that being part of a "community" isn't so
bad when you can band together to create a political movement
and find power in numbers to effect real change, like Stonewall
did or as the marriage equality movement is doing. Although
you'll still never see me and my girlfriend (or my wife) wearing
matching outfits!

As I think most people know by now, I don't like being told
what to do, especially when what I'm doing isn't hurting anyone
else. So, even though I am not a gay parade kind of girl, I am all
for a good public protest when we need to get something done. I
am not quiet and I am certainly not suggesting that anyone else
should be either. We all need to stand up for who we are and
what we believe in—whether it's together or on our own. It's just

that, personally, I would rather leave the lapel pins and bumper stickers at home.

I'm not judging anyone who likes a witty bumper sticker. It's just not for me. And, hey, the gay community has formed its own opinions about me, too—what kind of fabulous queen doesn't have a few things to say?

"You don't *look* like a lesbian."

"You dress so *fabulously* . . . for a lesbian."

"You're so much prettier in person than on TV . . ."

I have been out for years and I've even won awards for that, but still people say, "I didn't know you were gay. You don't *look* gay." Okay, so we gays are judgmental, too. Thank God everyone really is the same after all.

Some people cruise through life unwilling or unable to acknowledge who they are, and that, to me, is no way to live. Marrying a man when you really want to be with a woman but are afraid to lose your job, or pretending to be straight for your parents' sake when you know you love your best friend—I understand those are real-life concerns. But if you're disingenuous with yourself, you might as well be a zombie. You don't have to shout from a soapbox—although sometimes that is important, too—but you do need to own who you are and know you're okay.

You don't need to have a coming-out party or fly a fucking

flag or even march in a parade once a year to announce who you are and how you choose to live your life. You just need to be honest with yourself and hold your head up while you live your life the way you want to live it. Don't let anyone, gay or straight, tell you who you're supposed to be. The only person you need to make the announcement to is *yourself.*

THE FIRST TRANSFORMATION WAS MY OWN . . .

Here's me at five years old, proudly sporting an ABBA T-shirt.

At six, with my greatest inspiration, my mum.

At ten, traveling with my sister-in-law Viv.

At fifteen, a curly-haired redhead wearing equally bright red lipstick.

And just one year later, a platinum blonde standing with my mum at a major hair show.

This is my eighties look.

This is my nineties look.

My new millennium look.

Me with legs and new boobs!

And, of course, me now.

BACK TO MY ROOTS

Mum and I in New Orleans.

Me with my brother Gary and his wife, Viv, closer to home.

All the siblings together, including my brother Geoffrey on the far right, flaunting our birthdates.

On a recent return trip to Australia I visited the first salon I worked at, formerly called The Stud Bar.

On that same trip I visited with Lea Pratt, one of the coolest bosses I've ever had.

I wish I could include a photo of one of the many trannies from my parents' clubs who made my childhood so memorable, but the only images I saved are the ones in my head — and anyway, it's not my place to out them.

SUMMING UP THE COMPETITION

I'm definitely an Aussie girl as you can tell by these pictures of me with kangas and a koala.

But I am also a citizen of the world, participating in six to twelve international hair shows a year!

Mine has been a life of room service, sightseeing, and hard work with people from all different cultures!

Here I am in Hong Kong . . .

Greece . . .

and Singapore.

This is me at a platform show in Kuala Lumpur, Malaysia, where I demonstrated the techniques of a precision cut for the audience.

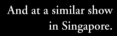

And at a similar show in Singapore.

On this trip to Bangkok, I was keeping a stiff upper lip after
having been mugged on the street the night before. Can you
see the stitches? Thankfully the hair design speaks for itself!

Achieving success is bloody hard work

The height of the experience is bringing out each person's unique beauty.

his business can bring out the best in all of us. . . .

Dating Yourself

- I am a terrific date and a horrible date. I am surly as hell in the morning and really quite accommodating when it comes to deciding how to spend the evening. I know that because I have dated myself. I took the time to get to know me for myself and not as someone else's girlfriend. Let's face it, we all change who we are for the person we are dating. And we can be different versions of ourselves depending on the relationship that we are in. But when it's just me, myself, and I, there is no one to hide behind or adapt to. And you start to figure out your own shit. I have a lot of friends who won't eat at a restaurant alone or go to a movie by themselves. They think they'll look like a "loser." But I highly recommend it. Take yourself to dinner, enjoy your own company, and make your own decisions. Tune out everyone else and actually listen to yourself. You might like what you find and discover some things that you didn't know you liked. Just don't start talking to yourself. That would be weird.

6

Idol
Dreams

I'VE ALWAYS BEEN AN incredibly hard worker, ever since landing my first paying job at my parents' strip club when I was eight years old. Since Mum and Dad had no problem allowing me to hang out with my aunties at Jeremiah's, it was hardly a stretch for me to work the stage lights one night when the light operator who normally did it called in sick at the last minute. The light operator's job was to run all the lighting and music cues, operate the spotlight, and open and close the curtain. He also announced the strippers as they came on to perform their acts, but Mum and Dad drew the line at a kid doing that job, so my father announced the girls that night. The lighting box was my favorite place to watch the shows. It was exciting to see all the strobes and flashing colors and I knew all of the performers' music and cues. So Dad handed me the gig . . . and quickly regretted it.

As one of the transvestite strippers went into her act, the tape concealing her tackle snapped and everything was in danger of tumbling out. Without any extra tape to fix the problem, she just wanted to get through her number, so she briefly rushed offstage and used the club's intercom system to tell me to dim the lights and keep the spot on her upper torso. That's precisely what I did, and as soon as she'd finished, my father blew the shit out of me, screaming, "Why the hell did you make the stage so dark? No one could see a bloody thing!" He was concerned that the patrons would be disappointed with a strip show where nothing much was revealed. But the stripper came back on the intercom to tell me that I'd saved her life. All the rest of the strippers said I was great, too, because I got really into the drama of the show and knew just when to bring the lights up and down and when to cue the music. But my father was not a fan and the light operator soon returned to his job.

Despite my career as a spotlight op being brief at best, it set me thinking about what I might do when I was older and I *could* get paid. From the time I was a little girl, I went with my Mum every week to get her hair done. And I loved the salon. I loved the smell, I loved the atmosphere, and I loved watching the hairdressers work their magic to transform people. The flaming queen who did my mother's hair was totally over-the-top—even to a kid who was raised in a tranny strip club. I never knew who he was going to be from week to week when I went to the salon. He was a rock star—his clients thought he was a rock star; the stylists who worked with him in the salon treated him like a rock star; and he acted like a rock star. One time he turned his head into a tennis ball, cropping and dyeing his hair lime green, and then shaving rivets into it like the white seams on an actual tennis ball. Another time he wore these crazy tartan pants and a huge tartan poofy-sleeved cape with a high collar. He was a supertheatrical diva and I thought he was fabulous. I wanted to grow up to be just like him—to be a rock star who did hair, too. So from the time I was fourteen years old, my mind was set. I would be a hairdresser.

Since I was too young to start any formal training, Mum walked into the Stud Bar, a salon in Surfers Paradise, where we were living, and offered me up as a free assistant so I could get experience. There, I got lots of practice shampooing, taking out rollers, serving clients tea and coffee, and generally doing all of the grunt work. This included getting down on my hands and knees to scrub the salon's tiled floor with a toothbrush, which today might be perceived as indentured labor, but back then it taught me a lot of things, including humility and respect—traits that can be sorely lacking in today's young hairdressers. My goal, of course, was to do people's hair, not to get down on my hands and knees like Sadie the cleaning lady. But I never lost sight of what I wanted. So it didn't matter if they were giving me the shit work and not paying me. I could already picture myself behind the chair as a hairdresser, doing rock-star hair. And I would have done anything to work toward that goal.

Located in the Lido Arcade, the Stud Bar was a very small, well-established salon run by two women, and because Surfers Paradise is a tourist area, many of their customers were vacationers. The result was a mixed clientele, with plenty of men's haircuts as well as a fair number of shampoos-and-sets and weekly blow-dries. Both of the owners were good hairdressers, but good hairdressing isn't all I learned from them. They taught me that when you have a love and passion for what you do, people will teach you things and give you opportunities without you having to ask.

Because I wasn't old enough to start my hairdressing apprenticeship yet, I couldn't style real clients' hair. I was only allowed to work on mannequin heads. But I watched everything the stylists did closely as I passed them foils and rollers, and I was such a quick study that ultimately they let me put the rollers in the clients' hair and back-comb and finish them. Eventually, the owners even let me do hair for some of the salon models.

It was a quick and dirty education and I loved every minute of it. I knew I had picked the right profession for me and I never looked back. I am not one of those people who floundered about, wondering what they should be when they grew up. I feel lucky and blessed to have known early on and to have achieved what I have in the profession I am so passionate about. I feel sorry for those poor sods wondering if they should go to law school or become a butcher. I never had any doubts about what I should be doing.

Raised in strip clubs, I was used to the excitement of a world where people were transforming themselves on a nightly basis. Once I started working, the salon filled that role. I loved the interaction with the people sitting in my chair. Watching their metamorphosis. Seeing their surprise at how wonderful they looked. Particularly with women, I loved the little twinkle in their eye that said, "Wow, I feel really good! I look great!" That was—and still is—quite powerful to me. It's instant gratification. It doesn't matter how shitty they have been feeling or how badly their day has gone, in that moment they feel amazing. And the hairdresser has made them feel that way.

The other part of what I loved about the salon environment was how creative I could be with myself. I could dress however I wanted—within reason—and during the school holidays I could also do crazy things to my hair without having anyone order me to play by the bloody rules. So, as I said before, when I was fifteen, I quit school—I had never been much of a fan of school and had mostly turned up to pass exams and get promoted through the grades. Quitting seemed like a logical choice at the time because I wanted to start my apprenticeship and get my hairdressing license.

In order to apprentice full-time, I had to move to a larger salon that could afford to pay me and was better equipped to give me the training I needed. So I went to work for a well-known chain located in Southport, a suburb about five minutes' drive from Surfers Paradise. Between the hairdressers, assistants, and receptionists, it had a staff of about twenty people. Initially, I was a "Saturday girl," and only worked on the day of the week when the salon was busiest. But I was such a hard worker that after a month, I was employed full-time. Whereas other apprentices were fresh out of school, my Stud Bar experience put me ahead of the game. I'd already worked for a year and I knew how to do all the basics of hairdressing and assisting. What I wasn't familiar with was the factory-esque atmosphere of chain salons, which tend to have a very heavy turnover of clients.

Dealing with such a high volume of people taught me how to be efficient with my time and efficient with my skills in order to keep up with the pace. After all, if I ran late and didn't get a client into a stylist's chair in time, I was in trouble. A timer would be put on and I would have to wrap a perm in only twenty minutes. There was a lot of structure and emphasis on not delaying the train. But rather than drinking the chain salon Kool-Aid, I used the experience to identify what I would do differently. For example, while some of the stylists were quite talented, they didn't have the time to do truly creative, innovative work because of the high volume. And customers weren't really taken care of because of the assembly-line churn. I knew I didn't want that for my own salon when the time came.

Because of the way the apprenticeship system was structured in Australia at that time, it took four years for me to become a hairdresser. It wasn't like beauty school in the States, where kids can do six months of training and take an exam to get their license. The Australian program was quite arduous and you had to really want to be a hairdresser or you wouldn't last. The apprenticeship consisted of working in a salon and going to technical college one day a week to do a lot of practical work, and learn theory, science, and psychology. But it was really the salon's job to give you your education and then you sat for exams at the college to progress to the next level. If you failed, you could actually be kicked out. There was a lot of study required to advance and graduate. It wasn't an easy program. I wasn't even allowed to cut clients' hair in the salon until the end of my third year.

At the time, when you did your apprenticeship, you had to sign "indentured" papers with the salon that employed you. And the program was overseen by the government to make sure you were trained properly at the location where you were employed. Two and a half years into my apprenticeship, I got fired by the chain salon and was in danger of having to put the whole program on hold until I could find a new employer. I was frustrated and devastated by the delay. I had gotten the rough end of the pineapple, and it was all the salon's fault.

There were over thirty locations in the chain, so they would hold intrasalon hair competitions where the various branches of the company competed against each other. I was asked to model at one of the hair shows staged in Brisbane. There, one of the stylists from my salon decided to cut and color my hair with really dark purple roots and white-blond tips—don't judge me, it was the eighties. I liked the way it looked for the show, but when I went back to work, my bosses told me it was too punk for the salon and I had to change it back to just one color. Since I liked my hair blond, the stylist stripped out the dark parts with strong bleach, which resulted in blisters all over my scalp and my hair literally melted off. I looked like a victim of a nuclear attack.

I started to wear scarves and headbands (did I mention it was the eighties?) to imitate Madonna and pretended it was okay that I was going bald. I was miserable. The blisters hurt like hell and my hair was falling out in clumps. All the while my bosses were telling me that I couldn't admit to clients what was going on because *their* fuckup would be bad for business. That really pissed me off. I wasn't causing a ruckus about my hair—it would grow back—but what was I supposed to do if clients who knew me asked what had happened? I wasn't going to lie and say I'd fucked it up myself or that I was the victim of a rare disease. So I told the truth and the salon fired me.

Hypothetically, without employment at the salon, I had to put my apprenticeship—and attending the technical college—on the back burner until I could find another salon that would hire me. But I was popular at the college because I was good at what I did, and I worked so hard that they let me keep attending class. This meant I didn't fall behind, and in less than a month I found new employment with Stephen Pratt, a salon in Surfers Paradise. He was English and had trained at Vidal Sassoon. His wife was a colorist who he'd met in London, and they owned the Surfers salon together, as well as another one located in Miami Beach, about twenty minutes away. Like the Stud Bar, it was a noncorporate, creative environment and it was great.

Stephen was an incredibly talented and passionate stylist. He could get lost in a haircut for three hours without realizing it. He always wanted to push the envelope and turn everything on its head—"Okay, so this is the structure of the cut. Now let's fuck it up by wearing a blindfold to do the same thing and see what happens!" He taught me that you needed to know structure inside and out before you could break it. Like Picasso, he could paint a perfect nude before he started rearranging the body parts on the canvas. Stephen knew how to break the rules because he knew what the rules were.

However, Stephen didn't like to say no to his employees very often. His wife, Lea, on the other hand, was a bitch—that's what everyone called her—and she didn't mind telling you what you'd done wrong and how you needed to do it right. She ran the business side of things. And she was one of the first "bitches" I really learned from, apart from my mum. While she would get in people's faces and demand a lot, she was also very fair. They wanted to have a team and they treated us like family. Her door was always open and there would be staff barbecues on the weekends. If you messed up at work, you were toast. But you were also always welcome in their home. Lea taught me a lot about how to be a tough but fair boss and I took those lessons with me into my career. I adored both of them.

Stephen and Lea were extremely encouraging when I took time off to fly to London for a weeklong hairdressing course at the Vidal Sassoon Training Academy. I was in the last year of my apprenticeship and wanted to improve my skills. I had also never been to Europe, so Mum and I traveled abroad for the first time, spending a week in Paris before heading to London for my class.

Vidal Sassoon is not only an icon and the godfather of hairdressing, he was my idol. The architect of the low-maintenance, ultrastylish, geometric bob that Nancy Kwan popularized in *The*

Wild Affair, Sassoon's cutting techniques changed the face of hairdressing. He created Twiggy's tousled locks, and cropped off Mia Farrow's tresses for *Rosemary's Baby*. Sassoon transformed a shampoo-and-set society that didn't really care about the cut into one where it totally mattered. In the process, the man himself became a household name, influencing and inspiring hairdressers around the world. It was my dream to study his techniques at one of his academies. To me, Vidal Sassoon was a rock star; he was the Mick Jagger of hair—albeit more refined.

When I walked into the academy in Mayfair, I felt like a Catholic entering the Vatican. Everyone was dressed in black, everyone was impeccably put together, and there was a uniformity of appearance and attitude that made it clear everyone had the same values. It wasn't forced, it wasn't contrived; it just *was*. Everyone wanted to be there and everyone did an amazing job. It was fascinating to me because, although I came from a great salon and worked for a great hairdresser, we didn't have the dress code and disciplined style of communication that was de rigueur at Sassoon. It was obvious that the staff had a profound respect for the man, even though, by then, he was living in California and not really associated with the day-to-day running of the academy. After my first day, I returned to the hotel and told Mum, "I want to be the female Vidal Sassoon." And I meant it. I would work as hard as I needed to in order to become a great hairdresser.

The class took me and the other students through all of the

classic haircuts. Working on models, we were instructed on what we were doing right and what we were doing wrong, and I liked that. Some people's attitude was, "I'm paying, so how dare you criticize me," but I wanted to *know* what I was doing wrong. I wanted to learn structure so, like Stephen, I could fuck it all up as a way of creating something new and bold. To me, being able to cut a perfect inverted bob was the Holy Grail because, once I mastered that, I could get really creative and become my own rock star.

I quickly realized that I didn't know as much as I thought I knew or was as good as I thought I was. This wasn't upsetting to me; it was motivating. When I went through the training at Stephen Pratt, I always thought I was good and people told me that I was good. But the class at Sassoon showed me that being good wasn't good enough. Having someone critique me honestly while showing me how to improve was a wake-up call to never be complacent with yourself, your education, or where you work. Within the week, I could see an improvement in my skills and an improvement in myself.

Sassoon's training showed me that constructive criticism is not negative because it helps you to be better. Trashing someone is not constructive. Constructive criticism is about tough love, as Americans like to call it. In my work, I always try to break people of their bad habits in order to make them better, not to leave them worse off. And the fact is, no one can be harder on me than I am on myself. I expect a lot of myself, and I'm the first one to comment when I screw something up or drop the ball. The realization that I needed to work harder to be the rock-star hairdresser I wanted to be was the biggest thing I learned at Sassoon that week. And the whole Sassoon experience made me realize that London was where I had to go to pursue my dream. I needed to get a full-time job at Sassoon and master structure so I could start to fuck it all up my own way.

As soon as Mum and I returned to Surfers Paradise, I couldn't wait to get back to the UK. I focused on saving money over the next year so I could make the move. I was working at both of the Stephen Pratt salons, going wherever I was needed on any given day so I could bank more bucks. That is, until the Pratts sold the salon in Miami Beach. Not only was I shocked when they off-loaded that property, but I was even more stunned to discover that they passed my services onto the new owners as part of the sale, too. When I asked the Pratts why they didn't keep me at the salon they still ran, I was told that they wanted to help the new owners hold on to as many clients as possible. They said, "We'd really like you to give it a couple of months so that the salon survives and we don't look bad. Then after that you can always come back to Surfer's and we'll try to find a place for you." In other words, they weren't getting rid of me because I wasn't good; they were getting rid of me because I *was* good.

I realize now that they had to do what they needed to do for their business, and business is business. But I felt incredibly hurt and betrayed. The whole thing really did my head in and I never rejoined them. I stayed at the new salon until I moved to London.

When I finally arrived in London, most of my savings went into a six-month class at the Sassoon Academy that basically had me doing my apprenticeship all over again within that compressed time period. I learned everything from the ground up, the Sassoon way—which was very precise, very methodical, and very structured. There was a way that one had to dress, a way one had to speak, and a way one had to section hair. Employees abided by a dress code and invariably looked incredibly well put together. When you worked for Vidal Sassoon, you needed to present yourself in a certain way and you took a lot of pride in that. When you turned up for work, you'd make sure that your hair was done and your makeup was on and your shoes were polished, and that really came from Vidal and his philosophy. It made me realize that perception is reality for a lot of people—when you put in the effort to present yourself properly, patrons do look at you differently. When clients went to Sassoon, they had an expectation of what they were going to get, and because the stylists spoke and carried themselves very professionally, the experience went beyond just getting a haircut. Those clients took us seriously as hairdressers.

There was no bullshitting about your personal life, and that suited me just fine. As a kid at school, I didn't tell my classmates that my dad was drunk the night before and wrecked the house or that I'd spent the evening at the strip club because my mum couldn't get a babysitter. I was used to not talking about myself, whereas many of the other stylists back in Australia certainly blabbed a lot about themselves. For me, keeping quiet was a natural fit. And Sassoon taught me that the focus really is on the person sitting in the chair, which influenced how I eventually grew my own business. Clients really don't give a fuck about who you went out with the night before or what you did on the weekend. They care about getting a great haircut, getting excellent service, and being taken care of.

A lot of people dropped out of the six-month class because it was hard. If a haircut wasn't perfect, we'd have to redo it until we got it exactly right—even if that meant redoing it ten times. And close wasn't good enough. The course taught me discipline and gave me the opportunity to get a job at one of Sassoon's Central London salons.

Although the discipline at Vidal Sassoon was great, I soon came to realize that working there wasn't creative enough for me. Yes, the training was exceptional and it laid the groundwork for where I am today, but being so methodical didn't leave much room for innovation. I wanted to start fucking things up and developing my own rock-star techniques as soon as possible.

It was 1988 and a lot of other hairdressers were doing really interesting things—quite a few of them were ex-Sassoon people. Toni & Guy, founded by Gaetano (Toni) and Giuseppe (Guy) Mascolo with their younger brothers Anthony and Bruno, were undoubtedly the new cool kids on the block. They were shaking up everything in the hairdressing world. They used the structure of Sassoon but deconstructed it to create looks that no one else was doing. Their photo shoots changed how people perceived—and styled—hair. So I decided to leave Sassoon because I wanted to be a part of that energy. And after I got a job as head colorist at the Toni & Guy salon in Windsor, I immediately had to go through two more weeks of training at their London academy to learn the Toni & Guy way.

When Anthony Mascolo walked into the academy, I saw that he was young, good-looking, and wildly confident. I was immediately attracted to him—not as in "I want to get in your pants," but as in "I want to learn everything you know." When we were introduced, he was incredibly gracious and I could tell he wanted to share what he knew with other committed and disciplined hairdressers. He soon became my mentor. Toni & Guy's deconstructed hairstyles were a lot messier, edgier, and more textured than those of other salons, so there was a whole new world of techniques that I needed to master. Anthony essentially showed me how to take my perfect nude and rearrange its body parts on the canvas.

The whole experience at Toni & Guy helped to unleash my creativity. While Sassoon had a strict dress code that included a black shirt and black pants, at Toni & Guy we could wear a black shirt and a kilt if we wanted to. I loved that edginess. My stint at Toni & Guy was a key part of my evolution and development as a hairdresser.

But ultimately, it all came back to that first day of class at the Sassoon Academy when I was still a young apprentice. I meant it when I told my mum that I wanted to grow up to be the female Vidal Sassoon. And I always hoped in the back of my head that I would get the opportunity to meet him and show him what I could do as a hairdresser.

That opportunity finally came in the most unlikely of circumstances. It was after I finished competing on the first season of Bravo's *Shear Genius*. I had been eliminated during a challenge where I was forced to pair with the one competitor who really made my blood boil. In fact, I referred to Tyson as "the weasel." Apparently, it made for great TV, but I genuinely didn't care for the guy, and let's face it, I am never one to pull any punches with my honesty. We were expected to style the hair of a bride and members of her wedding party as part of this challenge. He ultimately fumbled the updo he was responsible for, leaving me to do my work *and* fix his shoddy work too within a narrow time frame. We went down in flames and I let him have it right on national television.

So, of course, the organizers of the Stylist Choice Awards at the Orlando Hair Show thought it would be a brilliant idea to reintroduce me to the weasel in a mud-wrestling type of stage competition. We each had to re-create the finale of *Shear Genuis*—completing a cut, color, and a total makeover for three models in three hours. I didn't want to do it and had seriously contemplated canceling. By then, I had had enough of Tyson, reality TV, and the whole spectacle. I just wanted to be left alone to do great hair. But everyone told me that I would look petty and scared if I bailed, so I went onstage and did the stupid stunt. And I slaughtered him. I can't lie—it was satisfying, but only in a small and frankly slightly petty way. I already knew I was a far better hairdresser than he was. I didn't need to prove that to anyone (not to mention I was a better TV personality, having been voted the fan favorite on the show).

The real triumph came later, however, when backstage I turned around and came face-to-face with my idol . . . Vidal Sassoon. He looked like . . . well, the most refined rock star I have ever seen. And I won't lie. I swooned a little. Vidal stopped by to tell me that I was the first hairdresser he had seen do that quality of work since Roger Thompson, his creative director back in the heyday of Sassoon. I started to cry. The compliment may not mean anything to the layperson, but to a hairdresser it means everything. It means I had become the rock star I had always wanted to be. I will never be Vidal Sassoon—no one will. But that day, which started as an annoying lark with Tyson and a stupid reality-TV rematch, ended up being the day my dream came true. It just goes to show that you may think something is small and petty, but you should always give it your all because it could lead to something huge. It could lead you to your dream. In that moment, I knew everything I had done, every choice I had made up until that point, were the rights ones. Because they got me here.

Living the Dream

• It isn't easy to "live the dream," but for some people it's even harder to figure out what "the dream" is. I knew early on that I wanted to be a hairdresser, but if you're one of those people casting about trying to figure it out or saying, "Oh well, I'll just go to law school," then I have a few key questions that you should ask yourself:

• "What makes you miserable?" While this might not seem like the logical starting place, it is. You'd be amazed how many law school graduates hate practicing law. They should have asked themselves this question before they applied.

• "When you have a Sunday afternoon with nothing to do, how do you spend it?" Now, if your answer is in bed with a bowl of cold cereal, I can't necessarily pinpoint your dream—other than to say it involves Cap'n Crunch. But even reading the newspaper tells you something. Maybe you want to report the news or deal with politics. Maybe you like the sports page and will become the manager of the New York Yankees. And that brings me to my second point:

• Dream big. Leave it to others—whether it's your sworn enemy or your mother—to tell you something can't be done. If you have a dream, supersize it. It's healthier than a Happy Meal and doesn't cost you anything. Go after your dream like it's the biggest deal you have ever seen and treat it like a monster to be tamed. If it's easy to attain, then it might not be your dream after all.

7

My Very
First Salon
Takeover

FORGET ALL THE STRUCTURE that I had encountered at Vidal Sassoon and Toni & Guy—there was none of that when I moved on to work at another London salon with a talented hairdresser, whose entrepreneurial style at that time was very laid-back. When I first arrived there, the stylists rocked out when they wanted to rock out, doing their own hair in the salon, shouting from one end of the place to the other, and just making do when they didn't have the products they needed. After my two previous places of employment, it felt totally disorganized to me. And it was. Instead of getting into trouble if I didn't look and act a certain way or arrive at work on time, it was suddenly okay if I missed the train and showed up ten minutes late or went out to lunch and took an extra half hour to do some shopping. It was incredibly different, which was eye-opening and weird, but it was also liberating to get away with a few things, and soon I was becoming just as lax as everyone else.

That's when I realized it was a problem for me. I was letting my standards slip, and after four or five months I started to ask the salon owner why it was okay for people to come in late or leave clients waiting or shout across the salon. He was a very nice man and a really, really good hairdresser, but I guess he just didn't want to be the bad guy who told people what to do. Every year, he'd go away for three or four weeks with his family, and when he was gone it would be a free-for-all. During one of those trips, I finally thought, "This is fucking madness, I can't take it anymore."

This man permitted everyone who worked for him to have a key and trusted that whoever was in first would turn the lights on and get the place ready for business. Well, as it turned out, I was the first one there every morning. Before long I was also the one making sure the place was clean enough to open for business and I became the person who stayed later to ensure that the towels were ready for the next day, too. After taking on all this extra responsibility, I decided to have a conversation with him about how crazy the whole setup was. He agreed that he needed some help and asked me to manage the salon for him. Welcome to an early version of *Tabatha's Salon Takeover*.

This conversation wasn't intended to be about me becoming the manager. That's not what I wanted at all. It was more about drawing my boss's attention to the fact that when he was away, no one showed up until ten o'clock in the morning. The salon should have been open at nine. One of my colleagues frequently had his first appointments at ten, but he didn't arrive until eleven, so his clients just sat there for all that time.

The culture that I had come from at my previous salons required that we all reflect well on each other—the theory was that if I screw up, it affects the name of the salon and it affects the stylist next to me, too. That's what happens when there's a team of people who all work together. So when I became manager I really shook things up. I was a bit of a bull in a china shop, as I had never overseen anyone else's work before. This was the beginning of my tough-love boot-camp rants: "What are you doing, walking in after a night on the town, wearing the same clothes you wore yesterday with your hair in a bloody mess? It's ridiculous!" Or "How can you leave your client sitting there for twenty minutes while you go out and buy a coffee? It's bloody crazy!"

Everyone was taken aback when I spoke to them that way, as the salon owner had never complained about their behavior before. So when Dominatrix Coffey began throwing her weight around, a lot of people responded with a quick "Fuck you!" Most of them had been working at the salon longer than me, so they thought they were more senior and therefore didn't need to follow my rules. Some even thought they were more deserving of the manager's job. However, if they'd been really deserving, they would have been doing the right thing all along.

There were two receptionists, five assistants, and nine stylists, and I knew they were getting away with murder because, without any structural rules, there were times when I could get away with murder, too. So their pissed-off attitude didn't intimidate me; it just made me mad and indignant. When they would ask, "What do you mean?" or " Why do I have to do it?," I'd simply say, "Because that's the rule now. So, *fucking do it*!"

Since my management role required that I take on a heavier workload, I never thought it would provoke such hostile reactions. In my mind, I was simply doing what was best for the business, and who doesn't want the best? It didn't occur to me that some people were only interested in what was best for *them*. So when I hit them with straightforward logic derived from past experiences, such as it makes sense *not* to keep a client waiting and it makes sense to have your hair done *before* you get to work—I didn't expect such belligerent responses. But I understood it. The ones who lashed out were lazy and self-indulgent.

Standing my ground, I next had to deal with the good-cop-bad-cop scenarios. When I told certain stylists, "You cannot do this, it's unacceptable," they'd go running to the owner in the hope that he'd say, "It's okay." I, of course, didn't need these contradictions because they would seriously undermine me. So, again, I had a word with my boss and told him that if he didn't stick up for me when this happened, I wouldn't be able to work for him anymore. I mean, why make the effort just to get stressed out and be totally ineffective? *He* was the one who, having seen how responsible and trustworthy I was, had asked for my help running his salon so that when he took time off or was out of the salon on other business, he could be assured that everything would be okay.

That talk did the trick, and to my boss's credit he always backed me up thereafter. In fact, his wife once called me and said, "Thank you. What you are doing has made such a difference."

With his support, I was able to help the salon run more efficiently. He trusted that the salon would be open on time and that it would be clean, and he could also rest assured that the assistants were doing their job, the clients were being taken care of, the necessary products were always available, and no one was fiddling with his money. Still, it wasn't always smooth sailing. One time I had a huge screaming match with one of the male stylists in the middle of the salon when no clients were around. He went absolutely mental because I told him he was habitually late and had to show up for work on time: "Who the *fuck* do you think you are? How *dare* you tell me what to do!"

"I'm the manager and you'll do as I say," I replied, and the owner confirmed this when the guy mistakenly turned to him for support. Later, the same guy quit. He and everyone else knew I was there for the long haul. So they had to put up or get out. But there was still resistance all along the way, and whereas I now try to include diplomacy in my arsenal of countermeasures, back then it just wasn't on my radar.

One of the stylists had a raging ego that spiraled way out of control both with his clients and with other members of the staff. He was so high maintenance that it wasn't worth the effort to deal with him. He thought he could do whatever he wanted because he was so fabulous, and quite frankly he *wasn't* that fabulous at all. When he didn't want to tone it down and refused to be a team player, it was time to let him go. So I fired him.

"This clearly isn't working out and you're obviously not happy," I told him. "We're also not happy, so you'll probably be much better suited at another salon." When he inquired as to why we weren't happy, I told him: "Frankly, your work is crap."

"All right, fine," he said, "I'll pack my stuff," and off he went. He couldn't argue with the truth.

These days, instead of telling him he was crap, I'd probably point to our different belief systems and say that it just didn't work for the business I was trying to build. This wouldn't be quite so truthful—he really *was* crap—but it would achieve the same result in a nicer way. And as you know, tact is now my middle name—*don't laugh*—even if I do still vent my frustration when I'm passionate about something and people don't see the potential that I see. Or, even worse, when what they're doing is hurting themselves, their business, and everyone around them. At those times, I'm still the bull in the china shop.

After about seven months of working really hard to turn things around in that job, my efforts began to pay off. People could see I didn't ask them to do anything that I didn't do myself—if I asked them to clean, they knew I was also coming in early to clean or that I'd help them. So they respected what I was doing and I honestly think that they noticed and liked the difference at the shop They could see how things were now better organized and that the salon not only looked better but the clients were being properly taken care of, too. For my part, I loved taking charge of something and seeing the fruits of my labor. The business was in better shape, my colleagues had an enhanced working environment, and the clients were having a much more positive experience. This salon owner still runs a very successful business today, having branched out into many cutting-edge areas, and no doubt continuing to surround himself with people he can trust so he can have the freedom to refresh and build the business as he wants to. I must say that I am grateful to him for the opportunity to make some improvements not only in his salon, but in myself as well.

By the early 1990s, having confronted my own complacency

and having found the motivation to transform a salon according to the kind of rules and structure that I'd previously been taught, I was ready to move on—not only from that salon, but also from London. My mum had moved to the States, the British economy had gone to hell in a handbasket, the IRA bomb scares had us all terrified, and people were rioting in the streets over the government's implementation of a highly unpopular property tax called the "poll tax."

As things grew worse, living there became hard, but for me this was a good opportunity to reevaluate what I wanted to do and where I wanted to do it. I wasn't running away from London, I was running toward my next chapter. It was time for a change—and I quite like change . . .

How to Fire Someone

• Let's face it, I represent every human resource department's dream when it comes to my work ethic and drive, but I may be their worst nightmare when it comes to my candor. With that disclaimer out of the way, here are my thoughts on the subject anyway:

  • You should check yourself before you take any action. Have you been consistent in your feedback with this person or have you been too complimentary? Mixed signals are the kiss of bloody death, not to mention dishonest!

  • In your prior warnings, always keep your comments focused on how the employee is not meeting your stated goals.

• If your expectations have been made clear beforehand, then the inevitable won't come as such a fucking shock.

• As soon as you know it's not working out, make a point of letting the employee go quickly and with dignity.

• Have a witness present and keep your comments brief. Tell them they are not meeting your goals, plain and simple. Whatever the specific reasons are, that is the ultimate truth. Never make it personal, even if they try to.

• Have the ex-employee leave the premises right away. Fire-ees are bound to get fired up . . . and so, too, will the rest of the staff if they remain there any longer.

- In the end, they may thank you. Letting people go can teach them to respect rules and boundaries—and even free them to step constructively outside those very same constraints to do work they are better suited for. And you'll be happier, too.

8

The
Boob Job
from Hell

I NEVER THOUGHT ABOUT tits, or at least not my own, until I arrived in America. And then it was tits, tits, tits. They were everywhere—on TV, in the gossip rags, and in my face, or so it seemed. I was the duck out of water, and somehow it all came down to tits. Ass I had no problem with. In fact, my problem was *too much* ass. It was the tits that were lacking.

In 1992, I was ready to get out of England. Having never visited the United States, I had always wondered about New York. After all, it was one of the greatest cities on earth and an international hub for fashion and beauty. A little over a year earlier, my mother had remarried, to an American, and relocated to Ridgewood, New Jersey, so I decided to join her there. But I quickly realized that Ridgewood, an upper-class bedroom community, was not New York and it wasn't London either.

In suburban New Jersey everyone looked the same . . . except me. I was the weird girl with the shaved head and crazy clothes. With my anglicized Aussie accent, I also didn't sound like everyone else. And I certainly didn't act like everyone else. People definitely noticed. One of the first incidents I remember was ordering a tomato-and-onion sandwich in a local bagel store. The server made fun of the way I pronounced "tom-ahto" because he didn't understand what I was saying. After I kept pointing at the fruit in question, he finally exclaimed, "Ohhh, you mean a *tomato*!" What else could he have thought I was referring to? A fucking *nuclear missile*? "Yes, yes, a *tomaydo*-and-onion sandwich," I corrected myself, which prompted more hilarity because he thought it was such a bizarre food combination. How fucking provincial, I thought. The town was less than thirty miles outside of one of the most cosmopolitan cities in the world to which most of the residents commuted every day for work. Obviously, in the humdrum daily grind, it was easy to forget all the different cultures and people around them.

Another time, I was eating in a diner with my mother and laughing about the outcry that Sinéad O'Connor had recently caused by tearing up a photo of the pope on *Saturday Night Live*. "So what?" I remarked. "It's not like she stabbed him." Well, the people sitting behind me were obviously listening to our conversation and they decided to get involved by telling me how horribly wrong I was. They were the ones butting into our conversation, but I was the one being chastised. I felt like a frustrated fish out of water.

Shortly after I moved to Ridgewood, a woman in a grocery store asked me how my treatment was going. "What are you talking about?" I asked. "Well, you don't have any hair," she replied, "so I assume you're going through chemo." At first, I thought the stupid cow was being sarcastic, but then I realized that to her way of thinking, there couldn't *be* any other possible reason for shaving my head.

I love hair—*obviously*—and I enjoy working with it, but for me it's never been the be-all and end-all of what makes a person attractive. Yes, I think it's beautiful, and the right cut and color can definitely make a woman or a man more eye-catching. But you don't need long hair to be sexy or stunning. In London during the late eighties and early nineties, people were more open to expressing themselves with their hair, whether it was brightly colored, styled unconventionally, cropped short, or cut altogether—it was viewed as an accessory. In New Jersey, however, people were really uncomfortable that I didn't have any hair. "For fuck's sake," I felt like saying. "Stop worrying so much about me and worry more about *yourself*!"

My first job in Ridgewood was in a large salon, and because I was new I'd only get clients when they asked for me or when all of the other stylists were busy. That's normal in this business. However, some of the clients would say, "I don't want that girl with no hair to cut *my* hair." They were quite literally scared at the sight of me. Just as the children in school had run away from the fat kid, fearing my weight might be contagious, these women were concerned I'd inflict my baldness on *them*.

At one point, the salon owners actually put me in the basement, and although no one ever admitted it, I knew this was because they wanted to hide me. It reminded me of an incident when I was working for Stephen Pratt back in Australia. During a staff meeting one day, he told another stylist, "If you want to hide, go and stand behind Tabatha, because then I'll *never* be able to see you." I was mortified.

Confronted with such small-minded bullshit, I realized that the only thing I could do to be accepted was to show them what a brilliant hairdresser I was—*then* let people try to find fault with me! So I started to walk the boutique-lined streets, handing out business cards, and although some of the ladies fled, others were enticed by the free haircuts that I offered. Once I styled their hair, they kept coming back, and they paid full price and even recommended me to their friends.

When other clients saw the intensity I put into a haircut, they asked for me to style them, too, and the result was that I built my clientele from the basement up. What's more, within a year, I was not only on the main floor with a full book, I was also the bloody education director, training all of the other hair-dressers in the place! Ironically, *I* now had to fix all the client complaints. All of which proves my point that it doesn't matter what I look like; what matters is how I make *you* look and feel. I always knew I was a damned good hairdresser, and when all of those more conservative suburban women realized that, too, it didn't matter whether I was bald, fat, or a flaming drag queen.

But as brilliant as work was going, I was still struggling to find a social scene. In London, I had lots of friends and went out every night, but Ridgewood wasn't exactly a hotbed of al-ternative activities. It was a more conservative place with more conservative values. So in an attempt to fit in with my coworkers and clients, I started to date the NFL football player I mentioned before. There I was, never having watched the American version of the sport, and suddenly I was going out for fancy dinners with a defensive lineman from the New York Giants! It certainly got tongues wagging at the salon and around town.

We dated for a little over a year, but I can't say I was ever in love. I went out with the guy for the street cred and to prove to the people around me—who *so* disapproved of my bald head and everything else about me—that I could date the pro footballer that they salivated over. *So there!* Of course, I eventually got bored and wanted something—and some*one*—more satisfying than a guy who dated several women at once and clearly wasn't invested in me for *me*. I supposed we used each other, which is fine until it's *not* fine. The whole affair ended poorly, with me fucking up his Porsche, and that was that.

It was an accident, really. He had given me his Porsche for the weekend to get it detailed for him while he was out of town. In many ways, I was more like his girl Friday than his girlfriend. After the car was detailed, I was driving it back to his house. I thought to myself, "Fuck it, I'm driving a Porsche 911," so I put the top down and opened her up on Route 208 to have a little fun. Suddenly the bonnet, which the detailer had apparently not closed properly, flew up, dog-eared, and slammed right into the windshield. I managed to pull over but I couldn't get the mangled metal back down, so I had to drive the rest of the way pretty much hanging out the window to see down the road. When I got to the football player's house, I parked the car in his garage and I went out with friends in New York. He wasn't supposed to be home for another couple of days, so I thought I had some time to figure out what to do. As it turned out, he had lied to me and was away with a girl. When they decided to come back early, he saw his poor baby all messed up. I got an angry phone call demanding to know what had happened and I told him the detailer hadn't secured the bonnet properly. I could have been killed driving on the highway like that, for God's sake. He demanded $10,000 to fix the car and I told him that was what insurance was for. It was what you might call an irreconcilable difference in our relationship. And it was the last I heard from him. Although his poor southern parents still contact me every once in a while, since I am the girlfriend who moved them from their trailer into a house for him. In the end, it had been a fun ride.

Even after the footballer, I continued to try to define American beauty to help me fit in more. From what I could see, most popular American girls had nice teeth, long hair, and big boobs—they were *Barbie dolls*! So I tried growing my hair, losing weight, and—drumroll, please—getting a boob job. Small on top and big in the behind, I had always felt that if I had a little more up top it would somehow balance my arse. It was stereotypical female logic. God knows, most of the other girls my pro football boyfriend dated had big boobs—or at least bigger boobs than me. Ironically, while I took time to craft individual looks that helped my clients express how they felt inside, I let their opinions push me in the opposite direction. Even after having suffered the torments of the kids who bullied me at school because I was fat, I did what I've been telling *you* to never do—I let the masses tell *me* what shape peg I should be. They made me believe I needed to be a round peg.

Through my Aussie eyes, America was all about the picture that's painted on the outside. I call it the *shiny obsession*, because so many people here seem to be infatuated with the surface, the gloss. They aspire to be those unrealistically thin creatures who appear on magazine covers but who none of us can really look like because they've been airbrushed to hell. Neither Australians nor Europeans are like that. The whole time I lived in London, I spent every summer in Greece, where it didn't matter if you weighed ninety pounds or three hundred pounds. On the beach, everyone had their bras off, and regardless of whether their boobs were pointing up to the sun or hanging down to their ankles, no one gave a shit. Thin, fat, young, or old, the women were on vacation, getting a tan. And no one batted an eyelid.

In the United States, perfect or not, everyone, even the most beautiful movie stars, seem preoccupied with improving their appearance. It starts at a young age with parents paying for everything from plastic surgery to dental braces. Not so in Australia and the UK, where, if people's teeth weren't really, really bad, the attitude is "Fuck it, leave 'em alone." In America, it's hard to resist the pervasiveness of the shiny obsession. I started to notice the differences between that shiny obsession and myself more and more, and I stacked up less and less.

For the first time in my life, I made a serious effort to lose weight by working out at a gym and dieting, as I mentioned before. In Australia and London, I'd never really thought about what I ate. If I wanted a *chip butty* (a french fry sandwich), I'd have a chip butty; and if I wanted a Snickers bar for breakfast, I'd *have* a Snickers bar for breakfast. Forget healthy. But in America, that same food was considered an evil commodity that prompted outcries from my coworkers of "Oh my God, you're going to *eat* that?" I felt like I was gobbling shit off the sidewalk and soon the embarrassment made me cave in to the pressure and focus on the shiny obsession, too.

That's when I got a boob job. I wanted bigger tits, but not to attract men like my football player. I just wanted to fit in by looking more like the women around me and wearing the same clothes they wore. It was all about the aesthetics. So I did my homework and found someone who, reputedly, was *the* boob doctor. During the consultation, I told him I was a B cup and wanted to be a C cup, and I showed him photos of women's breasts that I liked—not overly large or fake-looking, just in proportion with the rest of my body. After the surgery, however, I was a full D cup. I was huge and I was shocked.

When I left the hospital, I was all boob. Everyone started talking to them! Men, women—it didn't matter. They stopped making eye contact and stared at my new, fucking obnoxious knockers. I went from showing them off—partly because I'd paid for them and partly because I couldn't hide them—to standing around with crossed arms. I was uncomfortable with myself for totally the opposite reason.

Not only did I find the giant tits annoying—after all, I wasn't getting any bloody attention, *they* were—I was also annoyed with myself for thinking that a couple of water bags stuffed in my chest could make me feel beautiful. Having hoped bigger boobs would get me into some secret bloody society of Barbie girls and serve as the magic wand that would make me happy, I learned pretty quickly that the whole fitting-in thing wasn't that simple and wasn't for me. And things only got worse.

Four days later, while Mum and I were in a shopping mall, I suddenly felt as if someone had kicked me in the chest on my left side. The pain was intense. Aware something was really wrong, I asked Mum to take me to the bathroom, where I discovered that my left boob had moved up under my arm. It kept swelling bigger and bigger, so when we left the mall, I lay down on the backseat of our car. I had no idea what the fuck was going on.

By the time we arrived home, my implant was up on my shoulder and I was in such excruciating pain that I couldn't even get out of the car. Mum called for an ambulance, and at the hospital it was eventually determined that an artery had ruptured and there was internal bleeding. The NJ hospital where I was admitted wouldn't transfer me to the NY hospital where my plastic surgeon had privileges because I was bleeding at such a rate that they were afraid I would die. Instead, they gave my plastic surgeon privileges to perform the emergency surgery in their hospital. Two days later, he had to repeat the procedure when, after I was released, the bleeding started again.

From then on, I had nothing but trouble. I was in pain, my breast was lopsided, and it was hardening. It not only burned like crazy, but I felt ill all the time, often to the point of passing out. Every time I went back to my plastic surgeon and told him something was wrong—because I knew what was happening to me wasn't normal—he told me that everything was fine. He became increasingly resistant to my complaints and, eventually, he turned into a real prick and wouldn't speak to me at all.

Still in pain and disgusted with my doctor, I sought out a female plastic surgeon for a second opinion. She advised me that the best course of action was to remove the implants and the scar tissue and to put in smaller implants because the ones the first doctor put in were too big. I was relieved with her diagnosis. Finally, I was getting a straight answer and some relief. However, a few days before the surgery I developed a rash, and then the skin around the original incision broke open and the implant started to exit my body. When I called the new doctor, she told me to come to the hospital immediately. Twenty minutes later I was in emergency surgery.

When she removed the implants, she discovered that the infection was so bad it had eaten through my muscle. She decided that the three-inch opening under my nipple needed to be left open in order to clean out and treat the infection. This took nearly three months. I had to work throughout that time and, at first, I wore a drain that consisted of a catheter bag. But it was difficult to move my left arm without the tube slipping out of the opening, so the drain was removed and I had to stuff several feet of surgical gauze into my breast cavity to soak up all the goo and pus. I used surgical tweezers to insert the gauze and pull it out. I started off doing that four times a day, then gradually went to three times, and finally two times before the wound finally closed.

It was an incredibly traumatic ordeal. I had lusted after bigger boobs for years and then they almost killed me. To top it off, I didn't even get to enjoy the bloody things! After I recovered from the ruptured artery and had the implants removed, the side that suffered all the complications was never right. There was scar tissue, which was painful, and the boob itself was lopsided, which presented a whole other set of cosmetic issues. My desire for perfection had actually caused me to be even more imperfect, and although I was glad to be alive, I was pissed off like you wouldn't *believe*.

That's when I sued the original plastic surgeon. Goddamn it if I was going to let that guy do this to anybody else. And frankly, my lopsided tit was also dying for retribution. The painful ordeal had made me realize it had been perfectly fine on its own and then he came along and fucking mangled it. I would seek justice for my left tit.

When I found out that he'd already had a couple of other cases filed against him and nothing had happened to him, I knew I *had* to take him down. That's why I spent five days in court with a jury. Of course, his lawyer tried to paint me as some bimbo who wanted big boobs to show off, and as someone who was in perfectly good health until I brought the problems on myself with my shallow desire to be more buxom. To add insult to my injury, the offending doctor's own testimony revealed that despite me having been very specific about the size breasts that I wanted, he had ignored me and purposely made them bigger.

As if it was something to brag about, he actually described his "overfill policy" regarding implants and explained that he'd made me bigger because women never really know how big they want to be. In other words, most of us don't know what we're talking about even when it comes to our own bodies. So his personal philosophy was to always fill the implants by 25 percent more than what the patient specifically asked for.

Several expert witnesses and independent doctors who treated the infection and other complications testified on my behalf to refute his ridiculous position. In their opinion, it had been a totally botched job. My surgeon had inserted implants that were too big for my breast cavity, he had nicked an artery, and when he'd done the emergency surgeries he hadn't replaced those implants. Instead, he kept reinserting the same ones that were already smothered with an infection.

And guess what—I won the case. The surgeon offered to settle for potentially more money if I agreed to a sealed record. But that would have meant *his* fuckup wouldn't be public knowledge and I wanted other women to know what had happened and be forewarned. In fact, I was the first woman who actually took a case against him to the jury, and since then that doctor has lost his license to practice. It's the right outcome and it just goes to show how we all need to stick together. Part of the reason why I got those bloody implants was because I felt judged by other women. But we're *all* in danger of getting mangled by a doctor who is a total sexist pig, and we're all in danger of getting mangled by a sexist culture that pushes plastic surgery as the "easy" solution to getting a "perfect" body. If we don't stand up for ourselves and for each other then who *will*?

Let's face it, even if you have surgeries and they turn out to be safe and exactly what you want, they're not natural, and what I came to realize was that there's nothing wrong with the natural me. Certainly, there was nothing worth risking my *life* over. The fact of the matter is, the bigger boobs didn't make me feel better about myself; they made me feel self-conscious because they weren't really me. It's like wearing that new shirt your mother gives you for Christmas—it's not you, and you're sure you stick out like a sore thumb, but you wear it to please her. Well, I got boobs to please my coworkers and my clients and the people on the street, and they wound up almost killing me.

Obviously, I was better off accepting my real boobs, feeling comfortable with them, and moving on. It was a lesson painfully learned. I had been right all along when I was working my way up from that salon basement. It's not about what I look like; it's about who I am. And I am a woman with a lovely lopsided left tit.

Ask Yourself, "How Do I Look?"

• I am going to give you one piece of advice on boobs: they come in all shapes and sizes. And that goes for noses, bellies, eyes, and every other body part that is now subject to debate in popular media. One of my favorite film scenes is from *Lovely and Amazing* when the struggling actress who is wildly insecure about her body asks the movie star who she just fucked to critique her naked body. At first, he doesn't want to do it because he thinks it's a trap. But then, as she slowly rotates standing in front of him, he tells her the good, the bad, and the "ugly." And she actually appreciates his honesty. And despite her imperfect body, he calls her for a second date—it's the movies after all! But seriously, we all could stand an honest critique of ourselves; you need to really look in the mirror and not just see the good, the bad, and the ugly, but actually accept all of it, too. Then plastic surgeons might have to get a second job!

It's Not Really About the Hair

WITHOUT A DOUBT, MY profession can be incredibly superficial because it mainly focuses on outward appearances. But that's often how everyone in our culture is perceived—bankers are supposed to look like bankers, rock stars are supposed to look like rock stars, and I'm supposed to look like a fucking lesbian! I just don't understand that. Of course, people have to dress professionally for certain jobs, putting their hair in a bun to serve food or sporting a Mohawk to sell their latest rock album. But when we get wrapped up in a certain identity, we often lose sight of who we truly are and we forget that our identity is always evolving.

How we're perceived or how we perceive ourselves becomes its own reality and we're constantly judged according to how we look. It's like the scene in *Pretty Woman* where the Julia Roberts character is snubbed in an upscale boutique by a snotty cow who mistakenly assumes she doesn't have a penny to her name. We make assumptions all the time based on how people look, especially when we don't bother to delve beyond the outward appearance to find out who the person really is. As a hairdresser, I've always tried to get to know people and go beyond the superficial perceptions so that I can help them get to know themselves a little bit better. And sometimes clients can have the strangest revelations about themselves while sitting in the salon chair.

I remember once when I was an apprentice at Stephen Pratt in Surfers Paradise assisting a stylist to apply color, I commented on the fact that the client was making a big change to her hair. She said, "Yes, I'm coming back into life."

"What do you mean, you're 'coming back into life'?" I asked. I was young and she was in her midfifties, so her statement sounded bizarre to me.

"I just got out of a psychiatric facility," she replied without batting an eyelid. "I killed my husband."

Apparently, the guy had been beating her for years as well as beating their kids. On this one particular occasion, he had grabbed a knife and was about to lunge at her when, in self-defense, she whacked him across the head with a blunt instrument, causing him to fall and head-butt the floor. Not your everyday salon story. But I went through the motions with her, nodding politely and going "uh-huh" while she spilled her guts. What else could I do?

"Fuck!" is what I really thought. "She's been committed for killing her husband, and when she gets out, the first place she wants to go is a hair salon so she can feel good about herself . . ." Not even a quick stop at the pub where the bartender knows her name first!

That was a defining moment. Suddenly I realized a trip to the salon could be about much more than just a haircut or dye job, and that the psychology is sometimes more important than the actual hairdressing. When people are going through shit, they tell their hairdressers secrets they won't share with anyone else, and often the revelation of those secrets changes the person and how they feel about themselves. It makes them feel renewed, like confessing to their priest.

These days, there are associations that work with hairdressers so that, if people sit in your chair and tell you about having been abused, you can contact a hotline to get them some help. Like a therapist, or the local barkeep, hairdressers are in a position of trust. We are transforming not just how a person looks but how they feel and, therefore, they want to tell us things.

Over the years, I've had clients who are covered in bruises tell me that they've been knocked around by husbands or boyfriends. I've also had them tell me they've had cosmetic surgery to try to save their marriages and that their husbands didn't even notice. These people come to an appointment more in need of divulging personal information than getting their hair done. I hear a lot of their private thoughts and a lot about their private affairs, and I've always taken this very seriously. What my clients tell me *stays* with me—so any of you out there who are reading this, don't panic—but it's amazing how complicated things can sometimes become.

In addition to doing some women's hair, I've also styled their husbands' mistresses, and at that point it turns into a dance—*I* know there's a wife and a mistress, but the wife doesn't know there's a mistress, and that's how I'll leave it because I don't want to get dragged into other people's private lives. I'm well aware that although I know some extremely intimate things about many of the clients who sit in my chair, I'm ultimately qualified as a hairdresser, not as a psychotherapist. There is a limit on advice. It is more about being a good listener and using my craft to try to make my clients feel differently about themselves and their lives.

There are also plenty of clients who would say that they aren't coming in for the armchair psychological purging and that they just want to get their hair done. But those clients can still have a lot of psychological issues that they are taking out on their hair. Hair is a very personal thing and people can get a little intense about it. I've had clients walk in with twenty-page dossiers about their hair—how they've worn it and how they would like it, all properly printed and illustrated with scanned photos of themselves, diagrams that they've drawn, and even diagrams that their *husbands* have drawn. When this happens, I know it's *so* not about the hair. Typically, the pictures are old ones that enable me to look at younger versions of these people and—as I'll ascertain by delicately asking the right questions—happier times in their lives. So instead of it being "My hair looked great when I was in college," it's really "I *felt* great when I was in college," and they actually want to re-create that feeling of freedom or youth or whatever it may be. It's not really about wanting the vintage haircut.

In such cases, I'll deal with the issue delicately, diplomatically, and honestly, even if this sometimes requires me to explain what I think is really motivating someone's choice of hairstyle. I want people to walk out happy with the haircut and color that I've given them, and if they're expecting me to reproduce some feeling or moment from twenty years ago, that's impossible. I didn't style them twenty years ago, their hair isn't the same as it was twenty years ago, and they don't look the same as they did twenty years ago. So I need to ask them what it is about the haircut that they still like, and if I think their expectations are incredibly unrealistic, I'll tell them; first, because I don't want them to walk around looking awful, and second, because I want them to love how they *do* look. And how they feel.

It's the same when a new client comes into my salon with a

photo of a hot model or actress. This isn't really about wanting the hair or the look; it's about wanting what she perceives as the whole celebrity lifestyle. So, I try to strip away the haircut to get to what the client is emotionally responding to in the picture. She doesn't want to look like Kim Kardashian or any other fashionista flavor of the month; she wants to feel beautiful or rich or whatever the picture evokes for her—just like my "aunties" in the strip clubs dressed to evoke a feeling for themselves.

The way someone looks can be a powerful tool in helping them redefine how they feel about themselves. When a mum moves to the suburbs with five kids, she isn't required to have a haircut that makes her *look* like a mum who's moved to the suburbs with five kids. But I've had mums come in and say, "Well, I'm a mum now," as though that means she has to look a certain way or that she has to limit her choices. But I'll try to make sure she doesn't feel the need to change who she is in order to conform to others' ideals. Honestly, I don't even know what a "mum haircut" is. Maybe she wants a cut that's low maintenance; I can do that, but I also want her to have a hip and stylish look that will make her feel beautiful every day, bring out all of her best qualities, and work for *her* instead of for other people. You're not dead just because you're a mother; you're still a woman, and it's okay to look sexy and want to have people look at you.

When people do come in for a physical transformation, it's often because they want to feel better about themselves, they want to be touched, they want to be pampered. Again, it's not really about the hair; it's about something much more emotional, and that's why I dig deeper. Certain stylists might just comply with a customer's request to go blond because they think it'll be fun. But by asking why she suddenly wants that look and how she thinks it'll make her feel different, I sometimes learn that the customer's husband has been having an affair with a blonde, and since he obviously likes blondes, she also wants him to like *her*.

It's interesting—when I ask my clients who they are, most of them sit in my chair and hit me with a litany of negative attributes: "I've put on twenty pounds," "I've got crap hair," "My hair's frizzy," "My hair's fine," "My hair's flat," "I've got a big nose," "I don't like my ears," "I don't like my double chin . . ." When they look in the mirror, they see themselves according to other people's not-so-charming judgments. And someone's look can redefine not only how they feel about themselves, but how others feel about them, too. So when I ask, "What do you *like* about yourself?" it puts them on the spot. Suddenly they have nothing to say. The fact is, despite the double chin, someone might have beautiful eyes, lovely lips, and incredible cheekbones, not to mention a wicked sense of humor. So I'll style their hair to accentuate those features, to make them feel better about themselves, and also to make them laugh about whatever they don't like.

Then there is the client who says, "I have a date tonight and

I want to look sexy." To me, true sexiness comes from within—from what you emit and how you feel—rather than from just how you look. So, once more, the outer appearance has to match the inner self. People with great bodies who are too done up *look* too done up, whereas those who wear T-shirts, jeans, and flip-flops can be really, really attractive if they exude an aura that they're totally authentic and comfortable with themselves. *That's* sexy!

Forget the old business credo that the customer's always right. They may be right in the sense that I *do* want to make my clients happy, but that's also why they're *not* always right. I mean, if a woman absolutely insists on something that I know is going to wreck her hair, will I still do it? Fuck, no. I won't ruin my reputation and I won't ruin her hair—"Go to someone else who *will* ruin your hair and who doesn't care, but I won't do it." Integrity is all-important—I'm really not interested in taking your money so that I'll end up with a few hundred dollars and you'll end up with hair that's a fried mess. That won't do either of us any good.

I've also learned to ask questions. One of my clients is incredibly adventurous with her hair, and when she got pregnant with her second child, she told me, "I want to cut my hair off. I'm about to have the baby and I want my hair really short."

So we discussed how she wanted it and I cut it. When she looked in the mirror, she burst into tears because she hated it. She asked, "Why did you let me do that?"

In reality, she didn't really want to have her hair cut off; she wanted something easy because she already had a baby at home and she thought it was a practical idea. But when she saw herself she felt fat, ugly, and naked because she'd cut off her hair. I didn't ask enough questions, I just did what she wanted. But she was having a crap day and made an impulsive decision. She is still a client of mine and now we can laugh about that haircut. But I learned that the customer is not always right. At least not when it comes to hairdressing.

When it comes to hairdressing, it is about transforming people inside and out so they like who they see in the mirror, even if they are getting the same cut and color they've had for years. And sometimes they want nothing more than to look the way they have always looked. Sometimes they just want to look and feel "normal."

Not long ago, a hospital near my salon called me and said they had treated a teenage girl who had just completed chemo and was going back to school and she wanted me to style her wig. She was a big fan of the show and wanted to look special for her prom and thought I was the hairdresser for the job. That is a lot of responsibility. She came in after hours so it could be private for her and we had a long talk about what she wanted in order to look "special." She was sixteen, and of course her biggest concern was that she should look "normal." She didn't want to stand out, and although her classmates knew about her treatments, she wanted to fit in and feel pretty like her peers at the dance. I got a really high-quality wig for her and cut it on her head while she watched. I kept it simple and gave her long layers and a heavy fringe. Despite being really shy, she came alive as I cut the wig because she was transformed. And she was thrilled with the result because she said it made her feel beautiful. Her parents were also there and they were incredibly happy when they saw the finished cut. Her dad even cried. If I had given her what I might have defined as the "prom-night special," it could have been a disaster. Sometimes, feeling normal does just the trick and that is okay, too.

With experience, I've definitely honed my ability to listen and analyze clients' comments. But it was my upbringing that taught me that everything is not as it seems. We have to delve beneath the surface to determine what—and who—is really there, and this pays dividends in a profession where we have the ability to make people feel incredibly great about themselves within a very short time. More than any other vocation I know, hairdressing is about instant gratification—if you have plastic surgery, it will take a while to heal and reveal the end result; if you have therapy, it will take a while to work out your problems and feel better about yourself. However, hairdressers can make you feel really good about yourself within an hour . . . or make you feel really shitty about yourself within an hour. And while the work is ephemeral, the feeling can last a long time. And it's the feeling that keeps a client coming back.

You can look in the mirror and say, "Oh my God, I love my hair," and have a little spring in your step as you bounce out of the salon feeling fabulous and looking fabulous, or you can look in the mirror and say, "I hate my hair, I look horrible," and slouch out of the salon feeling devastated for the next eight weeks. Let's face it, everyone remembers a bad haircut. I don't care who you are—whether it was Mom trimming your bangs, a stylist butchering your locks, or you having a drink, coloring your own hair, and making a right dog's dinner out of it. All of us, women *and* men, have that story of the horrifying fuckup. And by the way, the fuckup is never just about the hair either. It's about a feeling. And that's why it is so important to feel good about yourself inside and out.

The Five Things to Ask Yourself Before Opening a Business

- "Is this truly what I want to do?" You will live your business for the first few years while you build it up and get it going. So you need to love what you do.

- "Have I written a business plan?" Too many people jump in half-assed thinking they can make it up and problem-solve as they go along. This is how most businesses fail. You need to have a strong plan for success.

- "Do I have the finances and resources to back it up?" Don't spend your every last cent before you even open your doors. Say no to the extra fixtures or higher-priced paint and save for the rainy day that is around the corner. Unexpected expenses will come up and they will take you down if you don't have a reserve to cover them.

• "Do I have the skill to back it up?" I meet so many salon owners who not only don't know about hairdressing, they don't know how to balance a checkbook. There are lots of adult education classes that can teach you the 101s of business skills, and you should also know about the kind of business you are opening. If it's a salon, you better know something about hair, and if it's a bakery, you better know something about baking.

• "Do I have the passion and commitment to back it up?" If you aren't passionate about what you do, get out now. Period. Commitment is 90 percent of success. Wishy-washy doesn't cut it.

Going with Your Gut

LITERALLY PUT, GUTS ARE your bowels, entrails, intestines. Not so pretty. But I have to say guts are good—and I don't mean when served on a plate with salt and pepper. You often hear tough guys in the movies talk about relying on such gut instincts as courage and fortitude, and I take a lesson from them. I always regret not relying on mine, and as I get older, I trust those messy innards more and more. Trusting my gut has helped me to push myself and take chances. And trusting your gut may be the best inner beauty tip I can offer to any reader.

When I was a young girl growing up in Adelaide, I dreamt of traveling the world. And globe-trotting was certainly part of the appeal of being a rock-star hairdresser. I moved to London at a young age and then leapt the pond to America when I was ready for a new adventure. But Ridgewood, New Jersey, is a pretty sedate town, so I jumped at the chance to be a platform artist and educator for Joico, a major international product company, because it meant traveling to a lot of other interesting places. I would go to far-flung cities I'd never been to before and teach local educators a new technique or how to work with a product that the company had just introduced. I would also participate in hair shows where I would style anywhere from ten to forty models. I started out working domestically for the company and got to see all the bits and pieces of America that I had missed. I went to places I wouldn't have booked through my own travel agent, like Alabama and Tennessee and small cities across the Midwest.

When I landed in Little Rock, Arkansas, the only thing I knew about the place was the song in *Gentlemen Prefer Blondes*— you can take the girl out of the drag club, but you can't take the drag club out of the girl. On the way to the hotel there was a giant billboard of Bill Clinton, who was president at the time, and someone had fired a hole in his face clean through with buckshot. Welcome to the president's hometown.

I will admit, I had a few things in common with Little Rock. It has lovely hot springs and plenty of bathhouses (I love a good bathhouse). And Al Capone, America's most notorious mobster, used to vacation at the Arlington Hotel, where I was put up for the week. Apparently, he made Little Rock a gambling and prostitution mecca. And let's face it, gangsters are familiar territory to me. Nonetheless, I was ready to get out of Dodge by the end of the week.

Within two years, I was doing anywhere from six to twelve educational events a year in the United States, Latin America, Europe, Australasia, and the Far East. Eventually, I worked exclusively as an international artist, flying about 140,000 miles a year. I got to see the world and in time focused primarily on Asia and the Pacific Rim, which I loved partly because it is unlike anywhere else culturally, culinarily, and linguistically. While I learned just enough Vietnamese and Chinese to get by during my travels, being in these countries was definitely a foreign experience and that was both exciting and intimidating. I have more than a few war stories from my travels in which listening to my gut really helped get me out of a jam. A lot of the time I was by myself; there was no team. It was just me and the locals with whom I worked, and I had to follow my instincts if I wanted to do my job and stay safe.

I traveled to Taipei one March to conduct a weeklong training program with local hairdressers at a mountain resort. As I soon found out, March is typhoon season in Taiwan, but I didn't know that when I landed in the pouring rain. The drive up the mountain was very steep and my driver got lost. So what should have been an hour's drive turned into three hours slowly navigating the mountainside roads in torrential downpour with the driver screaming into her cell phone in Chinese. She didn't speak a word of English. We finally arrived at the hotel in the middle of the night and no one at the resort, which was in a rural area, spoke a word of English either. In fact, everything at the hotel was in Chinese and the rest of my group wasn't due to arrive for another day, so I had no translator. I managed to check myself in but couldn't get anything except Chinese-language programming on the TV. Even the room-service menu was in Chinese. I was up all night with jet lag watching the clock and soap operas I couldn't understand, and when it was finally morning I went down to figure out breakfast. But for reasons that are still a mystery to me, the hotel staff wouldn't let me into the restaurant— maybe because of what was to come. Oddly, I noticed that the glass windows on the front of the hotel were boarded up and the people in the lobby were thinning out. For a moment I considered following them to the exit, but where would I go? My driver was long gone and no one could understand me. It was pouring rain and I was in the middle of nowhere.

Instead of leaving the hotel, I went back to my room and tried the phones, but they were out of order. I managed to use pigeon Chinese to order some rice and vegetables from room service, but the hotel staff was nowhere to be found. When I returned downstairs, the place was a ghost town and the rain and winds were horrendous. I could see mud running down the side of the mountain and I knew I was in for it. The storm was clearly getting worse and I had no idea what to do. I couldn't communicate with anyone, couldn't get any news, so I did the only thing I could think of—I curled up in bed and slept through it. Sometimes you have to weather the storm, literally.

The next morning, I woke up and the rain had eased. I looked out and saw the carnage. Uprooted trees, mud slides, and sheer chaos. The hotel was trying to get back to business as usual and my translator finally managed to reach me on the phone. He told me there had been a typhoon and the entire area around Taipei had been in a state of emergency. I had essentially spent the night alone in a natural disaster zone and I didn't even know it. I just followed my instincts and muddled through.

My gut also came in handy when I did the first open exhibition hair show in Bangkok, Thailand. I had only done private shows in Bangkok up until that time and this was the first show where anyone from the public could buy a ticket, so it was a big deal. Not only did I do the hair for all twenty-five models, but because I was traveling solo, I made the decision to create the wardrobe myself, too. I knew the clothes had to be over-the-top; real in-your-face fantasy. During the last show I had done in Bangkok, the local stylist totally dropped the ball, failing to pull together any of the clothes that were needed. In the midst of that crisis, I wound up walking the streets at eleven o'clock at night with a pocketful of cash trying to purchase the clothes myself. None of the shops would work within my budget and I was ready to give up until I walked by a small boutique and saw a fabulous Thai gay boy through the window. On a hunch, I went in and told him my dilemma and he promised to find everything I wanted and get it to the hotel the next day. I was nervous but my gut said to trust him, so I gave him the money. The next day, the clothes arrived one hour before the girls had to go onstage and they were fabulous. My gut was right.

So when my gut told me to do the wardrobe myself for this big public exhibition, I went with it. It was a sink-or-swim situation—either it would be totally amazing or it would be totally disastrous, in which case I'd have no one to blame but myself. I can't really sew, so I drew on my experience backstage at the drag clubs for inspiration. I created tutus of varying styles: short ballet-type tutus, as well as tutus that were long in the back, short in the front and some that were covered in sequins and feathers. And it all really worked!

I had just finished fitting the models with the clothes that I'd made and I needed to get shoes, accessories, and a few other little pieces to polish the look. I was walking down the street in broad daylight when two guys on a motorbike drove straight into me. They were trying to grab my bag, but they also had a hold of my dress. So when they gunned the bike they started to pull me with them. In a flash, I hauled on my dress to get it back, but they still managed to take the bag before peeling away. I was lucky they didn't drag me halfway down the street. Only because I reacted so quickly did I save myself from being roadkill. But I was still bloodied up as I sat there on the curb. And I was broke, too. They had my money, my credit cards, my identification, my hotel key, and my cell phone.

I walked back to the hotel and got my passport out of the room safe, and when I told the clerks what had happened, they insisted that I report the incident to the officials. I went to the police station but the officers there only spoke Thai and they told me I had to go to another police station. The next police station didn't really want to help me either because the cops knew they weren't going to catch the guys. While I sat waiting for the police to interview me, an old Thai lady was being interrogated for stealing a bottle of shampoo. The policeman was screaming at her while she was on her hands and knees kissing his feet and begging for forgiveness. Eventually, she was put in a cell, which I walked by as I went to give my statement. My account of events was written in Thai, so I have no idea what it said. It was a very intimidating setting and I felt quite powerless. I could have easily wound up in the cell next to that old lady being asked to buy my way out. Thankfully, I was smart enough to have the distributor's interpreter meet me at the police station and so I was finally let go later that night. But I have often wondered what happened to that old lady in the cell next to me.

The next morning, I was backstage putting on a hair show for a huge crowd, which came off without a hitch. Everyone talked about how fabulous the models looked and no one had any idea that I had spent the night at the police station sweating bullets before resuming my search for the perfect shoes.

That wasn't my only scary run-in with the authorities in another country. I was the first Westerner, *and* the first woman, to do a hair show in Vietnam. I believe it was in 2002 and I was really excited to go there, but I wasn't sure what to expect because, after all, Vietnam was still a communist country and I was traveling alone to meet the team. I was told that if there was any problem at immigration I should make sure I had money for a bribe. So when I landed in Ho Chi Minh City and saw all the armed military at the airport, I was on edge. I didn't really see any other Westerners when I got off the plane and it was chaos trying to figure out where and how to queue. I actually got through immigration without a problem despite having a fight with two Vietnamese girls who cut in front of me. Of course, I got my back up and told them to go to the end of the line and wait their turn. They started yelling at me in Vietnamese and I shouted back in English until I noticed all the armed guards around the room and thought better of drawing attention to myself. Sometimes, standing up for yourself in that kind of situation means shutting the hell up.

Baggage claim consisted of a few guys throwing bags on a carousel and all over the floor once the carousel was full. The airport itself was pretty much a tin shed. I looked out and there was a sea of people on the street screaming out names and holding up signs. It was crazy and exciting all at the same time. I found the one guy in the crowd who had my name on his sign and he drove me to my hotel. As we drove by an imposing building with a helicopter on the roof I asked the driver what it was and he explained that it was where the Americans had abandoned his people—aka the U.S. embassy. That was the last time I neglected to read the entire travel book on the plane before landing somewhere.

Vietnam is amazing and like nowhere else I have ever been. There are people everywhere and more mopeds than cars. I would see four people and a chicken all balancing on one moped riding among oxen on the road. It was truly insane. To cross the street in Vietnam is to take your life in your hands. You have to have balls of steel. You have to learn to cross by just doing it; if you look at the chaos hurtling toward you, you'll freeze and then you are fucked. It is the meanest version of that eighties videogame Frogger. And I loved it.

I went to a salon to prep the models for the show, which was being held at the opera house that was built at the turn of the century by the French and is quite beautiful. Doing the show there was a big deal because the place is now a government building, so we had to get clearance in advance. Officials were scheduled to attend, and I was aware that if they didn't like what they saw, we would be shut down in an instant. Needless to say, I had to make sure everything was really good.

I started to prep the models with a team of local hairdressers. And I use the term "hairdresser" loosely because you don't have to have a license in Vietnam to cut hair. I was meeting them for the first time and, of course, had to communicate through an interpreter, so I did all the haircuts myself. I directed the team to blow-dry and do some styling, but I was pretty much on my own to make fifteen models look fabulous in the first Western hair show to be staged in front of a host of Vietnamese government bigwigs. In a sense, I was representing the West and I didn't want to fuck it up.

Around the middle of the day, a group of government officials came into the salon and spoke to the local distributor, who was also my translator. The men were fairly intimidating and everyone stopped working while the distributor dealt with them. Apparently, there had been a lot of commotion over a "white" girl being in the salon doing hair and they had come to check on us. Again, I chose to keep pretty quiet during the visit. And after they left, the distributor told me they were the "morality" police and they'd heard we were spreading propaganda. When I asked what happened, he explained that he paid them to leave. So much for morality in Vietnam.

The day of the show, the opera house was packed and I was anxious to make sure everything came off perfectly, which it did. None of the officials gave us any problems, the models were really good, and the crowd loved it. After the show was over, I went outside to have a quick cigarette and gather my thoughts. In front of the opera house a line of armed guards had formed, presumably to protect the officials inside, and I looked up to see a sign written in Vietnamese except for the words "Tabatha Coffey." It was surreal and very satisfying to accomplish something no one had ever done before.

I like accomplishing things that are firsts, whether it is something no one else has ventured to do or something that *I* have never done. And I always try to follow my instincts when taking on new challenges.

As long as I'm telling travel stories, I have to tell you about the time I went to Amsterdam to do a trend collection training for Joico's European artistic team. After an all-night flight, I went straight to prep the models. At the end of a fourteen-hour day I was exhausted and jet-lagged, as usual. It was drizzling when I finally got to the hotel, and as I stepped out of the car, my boot heel caught onto the bicycle curb, sending me face-first into the hotel steps. I knew before I lifted my head that I was in trouble. I just prayed I hadn't broken my nose. Instead, I had put my teeth through my lip, splitting it in two, and I had banged up my knee, as well. There was blood everywhere. My two coworkers looked freaked as they rushed me to the hospital. Ironically, Amsterdam may be a city filled with drugs, but don't try to get any painkillers in the ER! The first thing the doctor asked me was whether I was high. When I explained the situation, he insisted he would have to give me all fourteen stitches without any anesthesia. I begged him to give me something to numb me, especially because I was so tired and upset. But he denied my pleas. Two nurses had to hold me down while he went to work. After they finished, the doctor suggested I go score some hash or pot to make myself feel better. I guess that's socialized medicine for you. When I pointed out that I also had a gash in my knee, they wanted no part of it. I reluctantly went back to the hotel and cleaned it up as best I could. I woke up the next morning and got onstage to do the training with a giant swollen lip held together with strands of black thread. I looked like Herman Munster, but I powered through. A lot of the people didn't know what had happened to me, so they kept telling me I had a hair on my lip, or worse—they tried to pull the threads. By the time the training was done, I felt woozy and weak. I had to fly out the next morning, so a coworker took me back to the hospital for a follow-up. The doctor left me waiting and then insisted the stitches were fine. By the time I got back to the States, I was feeling worse and running a high fever. Because I had to leave for Brazil the next day, I went to my own doctor and discovered that the wound on my knee had become infected. She gave me antibiotics and painkillers—finally.

I don't want to make all of my travel adventures sound so

harrowing or disastrous. There have been a lot of extraordinarily good trips, too. One time, I realized that I was a few thousand miles short of maintaining my 1K status (the highest status) on United. So I called up the airline and asked where I could fly that used the required number of miles. I wound up jetting to Hong Kong for dinner. I landed, went to a restaurant, and ate my favorite dishes—barbecued pork buns and lobster with noodles, and flew home on a full belly. How many people can say that?

But by the start of the new millennium, having spent the better part of two decades working for other people and managing salons on both sides of the Atlantic, I had the gut feeling that it was time to open my own business. I'd never cared about this before, but I was sick of complaining to myself about how everyone else did things, so I decided it was time to do them my way.

For me, hairdressing is all about the client. So I wanted to establish a place where stylists could do great work and maximize the client's experience. To that end, I set out to create an environment in which the people I hired would be eager to show up and willing to learn. Uncooperative attitudes wouldn't be tolerated, and neither would subpar results. I wanted to attract customers who'd expect the best and not be disappointed.

As soon as I thought, "I should do this," I was on fire to make it happen no matter what. I always had a business mind

and invariably looked at things not only from a creative stand-
point, but also from an entrepreneurial perspective, so writing
a business plan was relatively easy. And the location was fairly
obvious—I had been working in the upper-middle-class village
of Ridgewood, New Jersey, for eight years and had a great loyal
clientele, whom I had come to know and respect and who had
clearly come to know and respect me.

Everything was falling into place and then September 11,
2001, happened. There is no way I can possibly make that mas-
sive tragedy about me or my small business. A lot of people
who died that day actually lived in Ridgewood, so the town
was really hard hit. In fact, they have since erected a memorial
in the village square. But at the time, the whole country was
crippled and the economy came to a crashing halt. I wasn't sure
what to do. Everyone in my life, as well as all the pundits on
TV, were saying things that should have sent me running from
the huge responsibility of a shop lease or a business loan. The
stock market plummeted. People were out of jobs. Everyone
was depressed. It was grim, especially in a community where a
lot of people were still commuting to offices with a view of the
smoldering wreckage of Ground Zero. I regrouped and made
the gut decision to move forward. My dream would become
my staff's dream and that in turn would become my clients'
dream. The truth is, the thing I am best at in the world is

making people feel better about themselves and their lives, and clearly we were at a moment when everyone needed a little of that. So in January 2002, I opened my salon, Industrie Hair Gurus. It isn't a huge salon and it isn't a superfancy place. But it personifies my belief system and my work ethic and that is what has made it successful, not the square footage or the price tag on the fixtures.

It's funny how a lot of people who watch my show don't realize that I'm actually a hairdresser and business owner. This is odd because the show's about saving salons. But viewers assume I am some kind of celebrity now who doesn't need to cut hair or run a business. The fact is, when I am not out taking over someone else's salon, I am in Ridgewood, behind the chair, running my own. That is what keeps me honest and true and that is why people like to watch what I do on TV.

One night, after we finished filming at a failing salon in Boston, I had dinner with two crew members at a steak house near our hotel. When I went outside for a cigarette, this big burly guy walked over to me and said, "You look really familiar."

I just smiled. "What's your name?" he asked.

"Tabatha," I replied, prompting him to shout, "Oh my God! I watch you *all the time.*"

Looking at him, I thought, "You are *so* not part of the demographic that I'd expect to be watching my show." Not only was he a rough-and-tough-looking guy with a Boston accent, but he didn't even have any hair!

"I own a sheet-metal company," he continued, "and I love you." Then he turned to a friend and told him who I was, and I could see the guy thinking, "Are you fucking kidding me? You watch a show about *hairdressers*?"

"Oh well," the friend commented, "she can't help *us*," to which the burly Bostonian responded, "Get outta here! She's got bigger balls than *we* do and she could *totally* help us run the company!"

The next thing I knew, he was asking me all of these business questions:

"So, how *do* you deal with staff when they don't turn up on time?"

"How are you so honest and able to tell people what you think?"

"Aren't you scared your staff might walk out on you?"

It was fascinating. Frightened to tell his staff what to do, this great big guy was asking *me* for solutions. But then, being afraid has never been part of my nature, and this includes all of those instances when I've gone with my gut and taken chances. Pushing myself keeps me invigorated and interested in what I do—if I got up every day and did the same things without challenging myself, my life would become really boring and I'd be in danger of losing my passion and my drive. That's why, although other people can push you, it's important to take responsibility to push yourself. I've never, ever rested on my laurels.

Any business owner who thinks, "I'm successful and that's good enough," is ridiculous, because the competition will pass them by. Good enough isn't good enough. As soon as you reach a certain level, you need to raise the bar a little, and that's what it's about for me. I'm constantly raising the bar so that my business keeps expanding, along with my knowledge and my professional skills. To do that, I need to take chances. Opening the salon was a calculated risk—I didn't do it without running the numbers, having a business plan, having a mission statement, and having the skill set to back it up. Sure the timing was a major risk, but I followed my gut and trusted myself.

There *are* times, however, when I have taken chances based purely on gut instinct without calculating the risk—such as diving into the world of TV—and in those cases I don't lose my nerve and I won't give up no matter what is thrown my way. I've never been scared of failure. I'd much prefer to take a chance and try something new than just sit there and say, "Shoulda, woulda, coulda." So long as I don't lose a limb, kill someone, or end up in jail, I can at least learn from the experience, and if it doesn't work out, I'll keep moving forward and do something else.

In early 2007, an L.A. talent agency that provided models for my work with Joico sent me an e-mail about an open casting call for a new Bravo reality show called *Shear Genius*. Hosted by former *Charlie's Angel* Jaclyn Smith, the show would pit hairdressers against each other in a competition to create the best hairstyles. A panel of experts would judge the contestants based on their technical skills and ability to complete each show's two challenges. The top stylist would win $100,000. And I certainly could have used a hundred grand.

The open call was on a Sunday afternoon at—interestingly enough—Toni & Guy in New York City. The producers were apparently looking for outgoing professional hairdressers—it sounded like me. The idea piqued my curiosity and appealed to my competitive side. It was different from anything I had done before—owning a business, educating other hairdressers, or traveling the world—and it seemed like it might be a fun new challenge. Without mentioning it to anyone, I followed my gut instinct and went to the casting call.

When I arrived, about thirty hairdressers all stood in line on the street. I knew a couple of people and started chatting with some others. I thought they were going through the line in order, but then someone came over to me and asked me to come upstairs. I was taken in to sit with the casting producers, who asked me a series of basic and banal questions about my background. And then they asked me why I wanted to be on the show. I paused for a moment trying to game the right answer and then just followed my gut. I told them the truth. It was something I had never done before and I wanted to try it. They asked me how I felt about living with other people and I said it would be disastrous because I don't like living with other people. My honesty obviously won them over because they called me back the next day for a longer interview on camera.

When I received the call informing me that I had been short-listed and would be flown to L.A. for a series of meetings, I actually said, "No, I'm not going to do it." Suddenly I started to contemplate the fact that I wasn't getting paid for my time, I'd be leaving my business, and no one could really tell me how long I'd be away because that would depend on if/when I was eliminated. I remember thinking: "What kind of fucking idiot am I to just walk away from my family, my friends, and my clients?" So I decided to tell the casting producers about my friend and colleague Anthony Morrison. I knew he'd be great for the show and would want to do it. And, of course, Anthony did quite well, winning the competition in the end. "Take him, not me," I thought.

"I don't know if I want to do this anymore," I told the casting producer. "It kind of seemed like fun, but now I'm not sure."

"You've come too far to just quit. You really should do it," he advised me.

At that point, my gut kicked in again and reminded me that I had said I was going to do it and I never back down, so I decided to follow the project through. And while I didn't ultimately win *Shear Genius*, I won something more valuable, which was a new phase of my career and my life. Competing on that show led to my getting my own show, which allowed me to travel the country helping failing salons. And I love that work.

The hairdressing part of *Shear Genius* was fine with me, but the rest of it was tough, especially since there was no privacy and no contact with loved ones. As a result, the Tabatha Coffey with whom viewers became acquainted was mostly pissed off. And I wasn't about to hide it, since right from the start the one thing I knew was that I had to be me. Forget the false smiles and fluffy comments. No one was going to edit or manipulate me to be anyone but myself—I wouldn't give them the opportunity. I didn't want to go home and turn on any of the episodes and think, "Fuck, I didn't say that," or "I didn't do that." Love me or hate me, people saw *me*. It was only one side of me, but it was real. Even though every reality show appears to have its villain, I never felt used in that way. When I was asked questions on camera, I answered them honestly, and if any of my competitors drove me up the wall, I didn't conceal how I felt.

Unfortunately, after winning many of the challenges and making it to the final six, I was paired with an annoying little fuck named Tyson. He and I were like oil and water. Talented but narcissistic, Tyson was much more competitive with me than I was with him, and that's because *I'm* actually more competitive with myself. My chief priority is to do my best and keep pushing myself forward, and so when our joint efforts fell short of the mark, I felt like I'd let myself down.

What really annoyed me was that he picked me for his team because, despite our clashes, he knew I was a damn good hairdresser. But then he fucked up the whole thing by not admitting his own weakness. For the Elimination Challenge, we had to design wedding-day hairstyles for a bride, a matron of honor, and the mother of the bride. Having won the Short Cut competition, Tyson and I were able to choose the bridal party we wanted to work with, and in our case the bride wanted highlights and an updo; the matron of honor wanted a French twist; and the mother wanted to have her hair blow-dried. The first two would be the most time-consuming, so I worked on the bride and Tyson worked on the matron of honor with the intention of us getting to the mother when we could.

I'm not saying my work was stellar, but I did give the bride what she wanted for her special day, and this was important because we were being judged on client satisfaction, technical ability, and how the hairstyles complemented the dresses the clients were wearing. Tyson, meanwhile, appeared to be struggling with the French twist. I kept asking him if things were going okay and he kept saying, "Yes, yes, yes, I'm fine," until there were only fifteen minutes left on the clock and he finally admitted, "I don't know what to do with this piece of hair."

When I walked over and looked at his work for the first time, the client's hair was totally trashed. It was stiff and over-sprayed, with visible pins; there was undone fringe, a crooked part, and a piece hanging down in the back. It looked, as I said on camera, "absolutely atrocious." So I jumped in to try to save Tyson—and myself. But quite honestly there was no fixing the matron of honor's hair. I was fucking pissed. Had Tyson asked me for help earlier, I would have been able to do more to salvage the situation and we could have succeeded together. But instead, we were going home. My gut told me so.

I'm not stupid. This was television. It was a dramatic moment when Jaclyn Smith asked me why I admitted to celebrity stylist José Eber and celebrity wedding planner Mindy Weiss that I had "seen better French twists from beauty school." My temper got the better of me and I told her, "I don't care for Tyson very much." The bridal party said they could tell we didn't get along, and I confirmed this by informing my nauseating team-mate, "I've never liked you." To be fair, he took it on the chin, but I wasn't going to lie, even if the public and the press labeled me a bitch for saying that "I really want to kick his ass." At least I was honest.

Ironically, the episode in which I was eliminated aired the day before my fortieth birthday and the next day we taped a reunion show in which all of the contestants talked about being part of *Shear Genius*. Clearly, viewers responded to my honesty because I was voted the Fan Favorite, won the $10,000 prize, and got a call from Bravo telling me that they would like to have a meeting.

"Sure," I said, without asking why. My assumption was that they touched base with everyone in order to terminate the contracts we'd signed and to say, "Thanks very much for being on the show. Now fuck off."

The reality was quite different. At our meeting, the executives asked me if I'd thought about doing my own TV show. When I told them I hadn't, they said, "Well, would you be interested in doing your own series for us?"

"Absolutely" was my instant reply because I was following my gut. And *Tabatha's Salon Takeover* was born.

Doing the show has been a phenomenal experience, and although I am teaching many of my hairdressing and business-owning colleagues valuable lessons that I have learned along the way—most especially, to listen to their gut—it doesn't mean that I am not still learning lessons of my own. The last story I'll share about surviving on your gut instinct is a doozy and it occurred in New Jersey, right on my home turf. I had just completed Season Two of my show and I was in Australia conducting press interviews for the Season One launch there when my mother was rushed to the hospital in the United States. She'd had a heart attack at the start of filming that season and the doctors were planning to give her a pacemaker. I was a mess, to say the least, and between the show, my travel schedule, and Mum's health, I had not been spending a lot of time in the salon. Neither was my salon manager, who is also my partner. And while we were out of the salon, some of my staff decided to have a go at my computer and, unbeknownst to me, take client information for their own purposes. Soon after, on a busy Saturday, one by one my staff approached me and told me they were quitting, that it was their last day, and that they were going to work at a nearby salon. Not only was I genuinely surprised, but I was hurt, too. Most salon owners will experience a walkout at some point and I am the first one to say, "It's business. It's not personal." But the fact is, having four key staff members walk out on one day, including my lead stylist, who'd been with me for fourteen years and who I trained and taught everything he knew, was . . . well, personal. It hurt not only my business, but my feelings. I had a good long cry and spent the night wringing my hands about what to do. But the next morning, tired and dehydrated from the loss of tears, I reminded myself that it is business and that the business must go on. The problem was, I had a salon with no key staff members. So I had only one choice if I wanted to keep my doors open. I started working eighteen hours a day, seven days a week. The only reason a client couldn't get in was because they *literally* couldn't get in—every chair was full and every time slot taken. And I was servicing almost every chair. My feet were swollen and my hands had calluses. I was supposed to be at the

top of my game and here I was back in the scrim. But I was re-
silient and that was important because my remaining staff was
understandably nervous and looking to me for leadership. They
saw their team and a lot of revenue walk out of the salon. They
were concerned for their jobs. And my clients were shocked and
wanted answers, too. I was honest, kept my head up, and most
important, I took the high road. Believe me, I had moments
where I wanted to lose my mind at their unprofessional behavior.
But I followed my own three-second rule *and* my gut, which told
me I would eventually be better off. Some of my former staff
decided it was okay to say negative things about me to clients
and colleagues. Some of them even wrote my longtime personal
clients letters trying to recruit them. But throughout the experience, I was gracious, and eventually, I did manage to rebuild my
entire team with fantastic stylists who kick ass behind the chair
and want to build a great salon together with me. The fact is,
unlike many business owners I have encountered, I don't view
staff as disposable. I view them as invaluable. Make no mistake,
if you suck, I will fire you. But if you work hard, do good work,
have a great attitude, and want to be the best, you will be on my
team forever. I will go to bat for you and I expect nothing less
than that in return. Having those team members walk out was
painful, but once again it reminded me that my moral compass
is strong . . . and that I will survive.

Gut Check

- Question yourself. When you aren't sure which way to go, ask yourself a series of questions.

  - What feels right? You have a moral compass. It may not be the same as mine, but if you live by it, you'll know if you are making the right decision.

  - Can I go to sleep tonight? Sounds trite until you encounter a truly sleepless night, tossing and turning because you're afraid you did the wrong thing. We've all had them, and answering yes to this question can help you sleep like a baby.

  - What happens next? Sometimes we make a decision in the moment without thinking about the consequences. But the consequences always come (see my three-second rule). If you can't live with the consequences, it's probably not the right decision.

• Once you've answered all these questions, you need to listen to yourself because you know what's the best course of action. Following your gut can spare you agita, so why not try it?!

11

"Shut the Fuck Up" and Other Things That Are Okay to Say

I FIND IT REALLY bloody annoying when people say they're scared of me. Scary is the guy in the hockey mask who jumps out of the woods with an ax and hacks the young lovers to death in their car on a dark night. I'm not scary. I'm just honest—and brave, I suppose, when I'm being honest in certain situations where most others wouldn't be. Telling people what you think isn't a bad thing; in fact, it has served me well.

TV didn't make me honest. I've always said what I thought, even when people haven't liked it. That's why everything I've ever agreed to do on television has always allowed me to be me. I've never been told to react in a way I wouldn't normally react or say things I wouldn't normally say. How people see me on my show is how I am in real life. Then again, my salon staff and the trainees from my Joico days would probably tell you I'm a little bit nicer on the small screen. I wouldn't disagree. Age and experience have taught me that it sometimes pays to get my point across with a measure of diplomacy.

When the Bravo execs offered me my own show, I have to admit I was surprised. I didn't see it coming, but I was excited to brainstorm ideas with the production company that had produced *Shear Genius*. Obviously, my honesty on that show had paid off, and presented with the opportunity to star in my own series, I wanted to do something that would really reflect who I am and what I am about when it comes to hairdressing. I have a lot of respect for my industry and for the integrity of the people in it, and I wanted to tackle the challenges that real-life hairdressers face instead of coming up with silly TV challenges like trim this girl's head into a topiary with these garden shears. So we came up with the idea to take over failing salons guerrilla style and "boot-camp" them into shape.

I'm well aware that some people refer to me as "the Gordon Ramsay of hairdressing," but any similarities to the fiery, foulmouthed British chef are coincidental. I am who I am and I am not trying to act like Gordon or anyone else, on TV or off. Certainly, we're both really passionate about what we do, we're both direct and sometimes politically incorrect, we have "funny" accents, and we both say "fuck," but this hardly makes us the same. I understand the comparison and am flattered, given how amazing Gordon is at what he does. But I couldn't be him any more than he could be me, so the comparison stops at the superficial. I just wanted to be myself and help struggling salons turn themselves around.

On my show, viewers have been able to see different sides of me, one of which is being a bitch when I need to be. Taking over failing salons and trying to turn them around in only a week is obviously part of a format that was made to work for TV and it requires me to work quickly. But I am not a fake or a poser and I wouldn't do the show if I didn't think I could actually change these businesses for the better. I try very hard to impact everyone who participates, for better or worse—which means that the show is a weeklong boot camp during which I dispense some tough love. It might not be much fun for the owners and staff when they are going through it, but most of them realize how different they are when it is all over—whether that's six weeks later or six months later. And I've been incredibly humbled by their gratitude, as well as by the amazing support from viewers.

"Thank you for your honesty. You made me look at myself."

"Thank you for telling it like it is, because you've given

me the courage to tell certain people what I really needed to say . . ."

One of my primary objectives has been to make the members of the hairdressing community feel proud of ourselves. So I've been particularly gratified when stylists and salon owners express their appreciation for the way the show portrays the industry as more than just picking up a pair of scissors and *snip, snip, snip*. At the same time, they are also grateful that I'm pointing out how we need to step up our game in the face of complacency and that I'm providing them with tips to improve their craft and their business. They see that I care, and their support has actually made me feel more responsible to the industry than ever before.

But the most unsettling responses have come from the people who write to me or walk up to me on the street and say, "Because of you I have started beauty school." Or, "Because of your show, I opened my own salon." I feel a huge responsibility to those people, so let me be as honest as I can be and clear it all up right now. To the people who announce these major life decisions to me and are serious about making the enormous investment of time and talent, good on you, but to those who say it like it is folly, I want to reply, "Shut the fuck up and listen."

It's still a TV show, and it still looks easier to cut hair and run a business on TV than it actually is in real life. Being a hairdresser and owning a salon isn't for everyone. That's right, you heard it straight from me. Hold on a second before you run out and sign that student loan for hairdressing school or cash in that savings account to build a salon space. Borrowing money to pay for tuition or investing your entire nest egg to start a business is a huge commitment, and you can't make that commitment lightly. So let me ask you a few questions to help you test your resolve.

Are you prepared to stand on your feet, usually on a hard floor in six-inch heels, for sixteen hours a day, listening to a client whinge about what happened to her last night while you figure out how to fix the fried and broken ends that some other hairdresser jacked up? Because that is your day more often than not.

Can you afford to spend $20,000 to $40,000 on hairdressing school only to earn minimum wage in an apprenticeship program that requires long hours of grunt work with no thank-yous before you can so much as touch a client? Because that is the career trajectory for most young graduates.

Will you be able to keep the doors of your new salon open for a year or more at a loss every week, not taking home a penny for your hours toiling behind the chair because it is all going back into the business to pay your staff on time and stock your back bar? Because that is the state of the salon business most of the time.

Sometimes I wish I had gotten to the owners and staff on

the show sooner so I could have asked them these questions and saved them a whole lot of grief.

Don't get me wrong. I love being a hairdresser and a salon owner. And I love the profession. And if you truly love it, too, you should go for it. But—and this is one of those big-assed *buts*—you need to understand the commitment you are making or you won't last, and that just makes you a quitter. I hate quitters.

Keep in mind, if you do decide to go to beauty school, there is a wide range of quality out there. You can take out a loan, often from a company associated with the school, to attend a beauty college, which may or may not be accredited, and they will essentially teach you only what you need to know in order to pass the state board exam because that's all they need to do. You aren't going to get a lot more from those places. Now if that's what you are looking for, Becky's may be right for you. But if you want to play with the big boys, you are going to have to go to a serious academy, like Toni & Guy or Sassoon or Paul Mitchell. And there are countless other good ones—I don't mean to leave them out. But then you are talking about more money, traveling in order to attend classes, and committing to apprenticing after you graduate. You are in for the long haul. And even then, it doesn't mean you are going to wind up being, or even working for, the likes of Anthony Mascolo or Vidal or John Paul Mitchell. It takes a lifetime of education and striving for excellence to get to that place. If you are committed to that, go for it. Take out the loan and buy your brushes and blow-dryer now.

But if you are not . . . if cutting hair just looks like it would be more fun than the dead-end desk job you have now or if you've always wanted to open a small business and salons look easy to run, then please FUCK OFF!

As you all know by now, I tell it like I see it. I am an honest bitch. And I really wanted to get that off my chest before I felt even remotely responsible for turning the whole world into beauty students instead of firefighters or doctors. Now that that's settled . . .

I take my job very seriously. When I walk in to take over a salon and I see the kinds of things that are going on, I'm genuinely amazed at the shit some people think is okay to do. I mean dildos in a station drawer? Roaches in the phone? Cameras spying on staff? At the same time, I'm equally gobsmacked that, while the business has been going down the toilet, the boss hasn't had the balls to stand up and tell the staff what needs to change or hasn't opened his or her eyes to see just how big a mess the salon really is. I'm emotionally committed to every assignment that comes my way, even if that emotion is expressed as frustration and anger. I get angry because I care about saving these places and making them better.

While incompetence and lousy attitudes are common factors in the business fuckups I'm asked to sort out, I'm always stunned by people's acceptance of mediocrity. To them, good enough is okay. When they don't give a shit about their job, it tells me they also don't give a shit about themselves, and that annoys me. It's even worse when they try to take the piss out of me or appease me. I *am* trying to help them and I don't need smoke blown up my ass in an effort to avoid change. Sometimes those people are better left for dead at the side of the proverbial hairdressing highway.

I have suggested to owners that I would fire some of their stylists because of certain things they have done or not done. But ultimately, anyone who has been fired has been fired by the owner of the salon. And this is a major moment of transformation because it means the owner and the staff are invested in what I am trying to accomplish—which is showing them what is wrong and why they need to change. Sure, the people who don't pull their weight know I won't be around forever. But because I'm in their face pointing out what they're doing wrong—whether this relates to their work or their attitude—it's really hard for them to ignore me. Let's face it, I don't pull any punches, and more than one person on the show has been really fucking mad about that. But frequently, those are the people who have never had anyone point out where they're screwing up. Or, if it has been pointed out to them, they don't know how to fix it. So oftentimes it is the most difficult stylist or the assistant with the worst habits who will change the most. And that is very satisfying.

Okay, so I'm tough and I tell people the truth even when they don't want to hear it. But the flip side is that I praise them and acknowledge when they do something right. I have no trouble paying someone a compliment—even someone I don't care for. And when I give it, they know it's sincere. I'm not the kind of person who holds people's hands, tells them she loves them, and pats them on the head for turning up on time because I'm just trying to be nice and avoid conflict. Fuck that. If all I did was bullshit, no one would believe a word I say. When I tell those around me they've done a good job, they can take it to the bank, and the people I work with all know that I won't blow smoke up *their* asses either.

On the other hand, if my girlfriend has put on thirty pounds and asks me, "Do I look fat?" I'm not going to say, "Yeah, you do." I don't want to hurt her feelings, and I never use my honesty to intentionally hurt *anyone's* feelings. But if we were going to an important event and while we were getting dressed she asked me if a pair of pants made her look fat and they did, I'd tell her.

Because I love her and I want to be honest with her to help her. Now, I'm not saying it would be one of our fonder moments or that I am going to get a big hug and kiss for telling her to change her clothes. But sometimes, you have to take your lumps for being honest because it's more important to help the other person than to avoid conflict. That's how I conduct my personal life and my professional life.

Brutal honesty doesn't have to be mean and that's why it is important to know how to unleash your inner bitch without being an asshole. Remember: **b**ravery, **i**ntelligence, **t**enacity, **c**reativity, **h**onesty. You need to be brave enough to stand up and say, "I don't like the work you're doing," or "Perhaps it's time for you to get another job." And you can't be too scared or embarrassed to assert yourself in this way because honesty is part of unleashing your inner bitch—you have to be honest with yourself as well as with everyone else, and you have to be honest about each and every situation. But being honest isn't the same as being mean and mean is not in my definition of "bitch." If someone says, "I don't like you because I think you're a bitch," I can understand that. But if someone says, "I don't like you because you're fat," what am I supposed to say? "Oh, gee. Thanks for letting me know I'm fat!"

I came up with the BITCH acronym after viewers resorted to such a "mean honesty" in their assessments of me on *Shear Genius*. I'd been brave enough to take on the challenge of competing against other hairdressers on TV. And I'd been honest enough to be exactly who I was while I tenaciously tried to be my best and win. But these qualities can backfire sometimes when they scare people. So I suppose I am scary after all because I am one big-assed, loudmouthed bitch. And I'm proud of it. And I hope you will be proud to be a bitch, too.

How to Tell Someone to "Shut the Fuck Up"

• Bluntly. Some people just need to be told to shut the fuck up. Unfortunately, not everyone has the common sense to follow my three-second rule. They don't hear the cop in their head and so they need someone else to help them out. And that is where you come in. Ask yourself this: "Would I be better off if this person wasn't talking right now?" "Would this person be better off if they weren't talking right now?" If you feel obliged to find a polite way to get the point across, then so be it. "Thanks for your opinion." "I'm good." "Got it. You can stop now." There are lots of versions, but when all those more modest phrases fail, you should know that you can always rely on my perennial favorite: "Shut the fuck up." Don't be fazed by the shut-the-fuck-upee's deer-in-headlights moment. If the stunned look on their face seems to say "I can't believe you just said that to me," then so be it. You have to believe that telling them to be quiet is the best strategy for everyone involved. And now I'll shut the fuck up on the subject.

So Why Did I Write This Book, Anyway?

THROUGHOUT THE PROCESS OF writing this book, there have been moments when I have wanted to rip my hair out (luckily, I know some good hairdressers who could fix me right up). Writing is difficult enough, but writing about yourself can be, well, excruciating. Believe it or not—and I hate it when public people say this—I am a very private person. And I encourage privacy. In fact, when I am dealing with my staff or the owners of failing salons and they start to spill their guts about their private lives, I will often tell them: "That sounds like a personal problem." And I don't do personal problems.

So why would I sit down and write a memoir?

While I have enjoyed living my life and wouldn't trade any of my own experiences, no matter how challenging or painful, my stories, and the life lessons I learned from them, probably aren't any more interesting than yours (and hopefully not *less* interesting!). The fact of the matter is, when we write or talk through our life stories, it gives us room to reflect and to better understand how we have become the person that we are. We can all find lessons in life.

Clearly, a big part of this book has been me encouraging you to get in touch with your inner bitch and a big part of that journey is being honest with yourself and others. I would encourage you to write down your own stories and use the process of writing as a way to be honest with yourself and learn from your experiences. Writing, whether it's a book or a diary or a letter, is a great way to look inside yourself and transform yourself—even before you sit down in the salon chair. And the more you know yourself and learn about yourself, the bigger the transformation you can have in that salon chair. Because when you know who you are on the inside, you can reflect that on the outside.

As you discover your real self, don't be scared to show that person to the people in your life. I don't just mean the new hairdo, I mean the inner discoveries, as well. Let your thoughts, your mistakes, and your moral compass be known more completely to the people you care about. And maybe the people in your life will take their own lessons from your stories.

Acknowledgments

I TAKE "THANK YOUS" very seriously. To me, the words have to be earned and they have to be meant. I am not one to thank someone for something that they don't deserve or that they should do without thanks; thank you is never false or empty for me. That said, I am not begrudging about saying thanks either. They shouldn't be difficult words to say when they are real. The words should come easily because you believe them. And if you don't believe them, don't use them. Thank you is so overused now that it can be meaningless when uttered. Luckily, the people in my life know me better. I don't say anything I don't mean. So, I would like to thank several people for their efforts in helping me with this book. . . .

To all those whom I love, you know who you are. I appreciate you more than I can ever put into words. THANK YOU for your love, support, help, and for being my rocks.

Heather Schuster, you are more than my EP, you are my cookie jar, and I can't thank you enough. To Mary Rector and Behind the Chair, thank you for your continued support and friendship. To Hama Sanders, thank you for the beautiful photographs and for making me feel like a super model! To Damien Carney and Nikko and Joe Suarez, thank you for making me look good and for being great friends. To Steve Fisher, APA, Sean Marks, and Robert Myman, thanks for the support. To Hope Innelli, my editor at HarperCollins, thank you for believing in me, helping me, and putting up with me during the writing process. You were an invaluable partner in this process. To Carrie Kania and Lisa Sharkey, thank you for seeing the possibilities. I want to also thank all the hairdressers out there, who are striving to make our industry great, and all the supporters of my show for your continued enthusiasm and trust in me.